WHAT OTHER EXPERTS ARE SAY...
ABOUT BORN 2 HACK

"Bill is one of the most experienced security leaders I know in offensive and defensive cyber operations. This is a great read and insight into the work we collectively do to protect countries and organizations around the world. A must read for those thinking of starting a career in cybersecurity, or an introduction to the field."

~**Stuart McClure**, author of ***Hacking Exposed***, CEO
Cylance

"This is a thoughtful and entertaining read for people outside the cybersecurity field to understand the stories behind the headlines and how we do what we do to protect our governments and organizations around the world"

~**Manish Gupta**, CEO & Founder
ShiftLeft

"Bill shares a broad swatch of real-world experiences and lessons learned that he and others have had in a truly diverse and growing industry. I personally took the path of building software products to improve the state of application security, a path that has been mentally and financially rewarding. Reading ***Born2Hack*** reminded me that I live in a virtual corner of a very big industry with lots of opportunities. Maybe it's time to get out of my corner and explore other things..."

~**Mark Curphey**, CEO & Founder
SourceClear

"Cybersecurity has become the number one concern for organizations and governments across the globe. Bill takes us on a fascinating journey with tales from the front lines where one can learn about this new battle ground and perhaps land in one of the most promising career paths. We are going to need a lot more cyber defenders in the future, and this book will get you there or at least help you better understand why this field matters so much to our digital lifes."

~**Vitor De Souza**, Vice President Communications
Cisco

"Bill's decades of experience, leading, managing, and coaching shine through in '*Born 2 Hack*'. If you're interested in entering one of the hottest industry segments around—where demand for experts far out weigh supply—or simply want to engage with it, you need this book."

~**Mike Andrews**, author of **How to Break Web Software,** VP
Oracle Cloud

"This book provides real life insights into what it means to be a security professional and the journey of building one's career in this space. Bill has a proven track record of building, mentoring and running top notch security teams providing cutting edge services. A great read to get started in CyberSecurity."

~**Amol Mathur**, Director, Products & Strategy,Cloud Security,
Akamai

"Bill has been an amazing and pivotal leader during much of information security's history, and his wealth of knowledge is one we need to capture. In '*Born 2 Hack*', Bill captures what it's like to get started in information security, and just how important our job is. This book is a must-read for both newcomers breaking into information security or veterans looking to reminisce on the reasons why they chose this rewarding career path. Thank you Bill for sharing your journey. "

~**Matt Bromiley**, Digital Forensics & Incident Response Instructor
SANS

BORN 2 HACK

BORN 2 HACK

A JOURNEY INTO THE WORLD OF THE WHITE HATS

BILL HAU

First published: 2018

Special discounts are available on quantities purchased by corporations, associations, educators, and others. Fill in the contact form for more details at www.born2hack.life.

TABLE OF CONTENTS

ACKNOWLEDGMENTS

I would like to express my gratitude to Stuart McClure, George Kurtz, Mark Curphey, Matias Bevilacqua, Ramese de Beer, Mike Spohn, Tony Lee, Vitor de Souza, Zheng Bu, Tony Cole, Mike Andrews, Patrick Olsen, Robert Coles, Paul Chichester, Manish Gupta, Andrew Dyson, Rahul Kashyap, Rasmus Riis Kristensen, Amol Mathur , Matt Bromiley and Yvonne who saw me through this book; provided support, talked things over, read, wrote, offered comments, allowed me to quote their remarks and assisted in editing, proof reading and design. Any opinions I've expressed and any deficiencies found in this book are mine, and mine alone.

Thanks to all my colleagues and clients who I have been honored to work with—without you all this book would have never have found its way to life.

DEDICATION

This book is dedicated to the following:

My loving parents, thank you for your many words of wisdom, hopefully you have a better idea of what I do now.

My understanding wife, thank you for letting me follow my dreams.

My wider relatives/friends, please find someone else to clean those viruses off your machines.

Finally, a big thank you to the unnamed that are fighting the fight to protect our countries/citizens from the badness that is out there.

0

INTRODUCTION

Chapter Summary

I traveled the world helping companies prevent and recover from cyberattacks, I learned that all organizations and governments are struggling to connect, recruit and retain candidates with the right skillset.

'*Born 2 Hack*' provides the bigger picture of how cybersecurity works, and includes my experiences and lessons learnt from the trenches. My hope is, that after reading this book, one of the biggest take-aways is that every cybersecurity expert has carved their own unique pathway into this field.

The good news is that there's no absolute starting point, so no matter where you are now, there's likely a way for you to get your foot in the door.

A twelve-year-old tucks her first cell phone securely in her jean pocket. Delighted to know she can now text her friends and watch You-tube videos, she is oblivious to the fact that her phone also connects her to the rest of the world. An HR director, working in the corner of his local coffee shop accesses his company laptop from an unsecured public wireless network to assess performance reviews. The head of a developed country swipes through the news on the latest premium smart-phone, equipped with a camera and microphone, having refused to download any sophisticated software to protect the device.

Not unlike most of the four billion internet users around the world, these people see nothing concerning or even unusual about their actions[1]. Such online behavior is quite common, according to today's online activity standards. Consumers focus on connectivity, the speed and quality of connected internet access, and how it makes their lives more efficient. By these same standards, we know that they're taking significant cybersecurity risks that can compromise their identity and personal data and potentially alter their lives for the worse.

In 2018, over half the world's population is active on the internet and 3.3 billion use social media. (Almost) everyone— individuals, organizations, and government agencies—is vulnerable to cybercrime[2]. Stories of breaches regularly make the evening news; it is no secret that we are fighting an invisible, silent war that makes no distinction between age, race, or socioeconomic status.

Global cybercrime cost $105.45 billion in 2015 and is projected to reach $181.77 billion by 2021. Things will only get worse as countries capitalize on the growth a digital economy promises. Commercial giants and governments around the world fight threat actors daily[3]. However, even these influential organizations are often too late. It can take weeks, months, and even years to recover from far-reaching attacks that are typically unseen, unheard, and not trackable. Even Warren Buffet thinks that cyberattacks are now the biggest threat to mankind, more so than nuclear weapons.

The cybersecurity market has grown exponentially to meet the demands of government regulations and to defend against and respond to cyber threats. Despite the clear need for better prevention and recovery methods, a chronic shortage of qualified cybersecurity experts will grow significantly over the next few years as the number of breaches and their level of sophistication grows. Mainstream media rarely addresses cybersecurity issues. Furthermore, too few high school graduates and college students know that cybersecurity is a viable career path. Anyone who chooses this path can earn a great living with exciting travel opportunities and job satisfaction.

When I started out, there were very few books to guide those of us who were curious about this industry and not nearly enough mentors to hit up for advice. As I traveled the world helping companies prevent and recover from cyberattacks, I learned that organizations and governments are struggling to connect, recruit, and retain candidates with the right skillset.

Today, many of my colleagues and I are happy to help guide anyone thinking of pursuing cybersecurity, but there's still a considerable lack of awareness at the educational, continuing education, and professional levels. I wrote this book to help those interested in this career and to open their eyes to this growing opportunity.

Everyone writing a book on cybersecurity is, in their own way, helping to demystify and find ways to invite others to be part of this profession. Many of the published books focus on the how-to series, e.g. how to become an expert hacker of a specific platform. These are useful technical books. *Born 2 Hack* shares the bigger picture of how cybersecurity works, and includes my experiences and lessons learned from the trenches.

My hope is that, after reading this book, you, an aspiring cybersecurity expert, are able to carve your unique pathway into this field. This book is for anyone who has an interest in cyber-security and who wants to know who the players are, but isn't sure how to start. The good news is that there's no absolute starting point, so no matter where you are now, there's likely a way for you to get your foot in the door.

How to read this book

In chapters 1 and 2, I describe how cybersecurity came into being, how it led to my career in a field that never existed, and where we are now.

In chapters 3, 4 and 5, I differentiate "white hats" from "black hats" (hackers) and detail why consumers, businesses and governments urgently need cybersecurity experts. Along the way, I offer best practices that help protect people and organizations from being compromised.

The final section, chapters 6, 7, and 8, outlines how aspiring "white hats" can begin their journey, no matter where their starting point might be. They can also be inspired by other successful experts in carving their own careers. Finally, I offer my closing thoughts, what latest technologies will impact cybersecurity, and where ethical hackers have even more opportunities.

Throughout the book, I share my stories—the good, the bad, and the strange—some of which are detailed and openly discussed in the press, while others are modified to protect the innocent. I've also outlined some of the biggest and documented cybersecurity investigations as use cases to help you better understand what we're facing.

Who this book is for

I offer something of interest in this book for everyone, regardless of your level of expertise:

- for "budding" cybersecurity candidates—how to get into cybersecurity.

- for "curious" citizens—what is cybersecurity?

- for "experienced" professionals—how to make pathways and deepen your career.

Feel free to delve into the chapters that you deem most relevant. However, I hope and sincerely recommend that you read this book in detail. Stick with me, and let this book help you demystify the inner workings of the cybersecurity industry and how you can carve your very own trail.

Endnotes
1. According to the 2018 Global Digital Report more than two thirds of the world's population has a mobile phone, that is 5.1billion people, and it is also the
preferred choice for going online.
2. Cybercrime is defined as a crime in which a computer (or a connected device) is either
the object of the crime or is used as a tool to commit an offense.
3. Threat actors are cyber criminals; individual(s) who form the threat and are classified
according to the severity of the threat posed (see Chapter 3).

1

HOW DID I-WE GET HERE?

Chapter Summary

Technological advances have made the internet more readily accessible and available to everyone, and hackers see weaknesses in the networks and the code itself and take this as an opportunity to test their mettle.

In its plainest form, hacking, from a security point of view, is the unauthorized access of a computer system.

Hackers are increasingly more sophisticated and they will adapt to infiltrate systems and get what they want, without a second thought to their victims.

For aspiring "white hats" like you, it means having the opportunity to flex your technical, problem-solving, and communication skills. This means being one step ahead of the bad guys while staying cool under pressure.

"Everyone on your team must surrender their passports to me."

At least our point of contact spoke English.

But the senior executive wasn't letting up. "Everyone on your team must surrender their passports to me."

I refused. The first rule of travel is you never give up your passport.

"Why do you need them? We're here to help you, aren't we? We're not terrorists or anything." I wasn't letting up either, so we continued to argue. Ten minutes later, thinking I had the upper hand, I went on.

"Well, you know, we can go back home if that's what you want." And that should've ended it. It was already nighttime in Saudi Arabia, and the atmosphere was hot. I was fine leaving the heat early.

"Bill, don't worry, we'll stop you at the airport on your way home anyway. You keep your passports," he said, only half-jokingly.

Shit.

They could keep us from leaving the country whether we had passports or not.

Did they not know that local companies occasionally get burned because foreign companies made promises they didn't keep? Furthermore, cybersecurity experts aren't spies. We try not to fly too much into hot spots, but sometimes that's where the action is.

This was a serious deal. The client was not only one of the world's largest companies by revenue but also one of the most valuable. This was the first case of cyber-warfare in the commercial sector. It was the first time an infiltrator had accessed and destroyed a large proportion of the IT infrastructure environment of a massive organization using the Shamoon virus attack. It wiped out tens of thousands of computers and replaced the data with a partial image of a burning American flag. Leon E. Panetta, the then-United States defense secretary, said the attack could be a harbinger, that "an aggressor nation or extremist group could use these kinds of cyber tools to gain control of critical switches." Our mission was to figure out who was attacking them, what they were after, locate any forensic evidence, and help them recover[1].

My assignment took me to Dammam, Saudi Arabia, four hundred kilometers from Riyadh. It was my first trip to the Middle East, and I didn't speak the language. It was also during the time of the Arab Spring, which meant heightened security.

I spotted a driver who motioned me to get in the car. I agreed—even though the name on the sign he held up wasn't quite mine because it was misspelled. An hour later, I wondered if I was actually in the right car as we hurtled down the pitch-black freeway and swerved past a herd of camels. *The road lights weren't even on.* If only one member from my team were there with me, I'd feel less anxious. But since we were spread out all over the globe, we had all landed separately, each one taking a hired car along the same road, and perhaps, past the same camels to get to the command center.

By the time I reached the client's site, half the team of around fifteen was already setting up in response to the company's call. We worked in the command center over the next few months, sixteen to eighteen hours day to diagnose, analyze, and test to find the culprit, and helped the client secure its infrastructure. We were protected by guards, escorting us to and from our rooms with our passports intact. Surrounding countries were also experiencing similar instability. This meant that the attack could've been done by an insider, so these guards were armed. And if it turned out not to be an inside job but something else, military airplanes flew around the compound to protect it. While we all collectively learned a lot from this incident, most importantly the client recovered from the event, and I was impressed how they then went on to build a world-class security operations center.

I continue to perform infrastructure security around the world from the Nordics, Egypt, Turkey, and the European Union, the USA around to Japan, Philippines, and Australia. While I have yet to experience the level of IT infrastructure devastation as I did in Saudi Arabia, I find nothing surprises me anymore.

Hacking and exposing vulnerabilities

The internet has been around since 1983; it took roughly another sixteen years to become mainstream. Back then, (if you're old enough to remember), many of us used it at work to receive and forward jokes to friends and colleagues. Now, of course, we use the internet to shop, bank, find a dinner date, file taxes, and enroll in school. Today, millions of online transactions are performed every twenty seconds, and over 269 billion business and consumer emails are sent and received every day. In a short time, we've gone from using it as a small part of our daily work tasks to faithfully relying on it as a transmitter of information.

Technological advances have made the internet more readily accessible and available to everyone. Some savvy computer users saw weaknesses in networks and the code itself and took this as an opportunity to test their mettle. It did not necessarily start as a harmful act, but soon enough, some also discovered they could make a lot of money by stealing identities, information, or... money.

Here's where hacking comes in. In its plainest form, from a security point of view, hacking is the unauthorized access of a computer system. Hackers essentially test hardware and software to understand and exploit any weaknesses in a system and gain access. They then may go on to commit cybercrimes. While most of us use the internet for well-meaning purposes, hackers use it as their playground where they can access, share, steal or delete data, steal identities or login information, or spread viruses.

Hackers give "white hats" like me an opportunity to get in and fix what's broken after the fact through forensic investigation. We also help prevent attacks through ethical hacking and penetration testing[2]. We'll delve deeper into these disciplines in later chapters, but for now, just know that the internet means different things to different people.

People, the weakest link

The internet was originally designed as a closed "network of networks" for scientists to share data. It was not built with security in mind. Once it became an open network, the internet—and especially social media—made it possible to collect, store, analyze, and share a lot of our personal data and information. Naturally, big data and the infrastructure it resides in are very attractive resources to hackers. They can't help themselves from creating chaos, and this is what makes us vulnerable. According to the Ponemon Institute, malicious or criminal attacks accounted for 47 percent of data breaches in 2017, followed by human error and system glitches.

The question is: when did it start?

The answer is: we have *always* been vulnerable.

From my experience there are many reasons why we are defenseless against hackers, I shall talk about three that come to mind.

1. Some companies have **little or no visibility** of the problem. Certain organizations sometimes don't know what they don't know. They're content in trying to secure the basics in their infrastructure, and like an ostrich, bury their heads in the sand.

2. Others have a **casual attitude** toward cybersecurity, so it's easy to see how criminal attacks happen almost twice as frequently as human error or system glitches.

3. Lastly, **the cost of securing** an organization's infrastructure sometimes prevents them from fully protecting themelves, and those that are breached once will be breached again.

But here's the twist: even when the cost isn't prohibitive, organizations often still don't cover even the basics. Unfortunately, many of them operate without updated antivirus protection that requires only a signature update to avoid a computer virus infection. It's sometimes the basic-level hygiene that companies don't pay attention to that will eventually breed more significant problems.

In 2011, Sony sued George "geohot" Hotz after he broke into the PlayStation 3 video game console and published its root keys on is website. In revenge for the lawsuit, the hacking community went after Sony. It was one of the first major publicly acknowledged cases where a congregation of hackers with a common cause got together to outdo big business. They exploited a trivial yet glaring security vulnerability that had been known for a long time and should have been fixed. Through an SQL-injection attack[3], the group broke into Sony's PlayStation Network, its streaming media service–Qriocity, and its game developer and publisher–Sony Online Entertainment. The group exposed the personal data of some 77 million customers in the biggest gaming hack to date. PlayStation as again breached in October that year. I know what you're thinking: company with pockets as deep as Sony's should be able to better protect themselves, right?

Certainly, an attack surface[4] like Sony's is so large that a proper integrated risk assessment may not have been performed to deploy appropriate technical countermeasures and remediate vulnerabilities. Furthermore, the then-senior leaders of the organization may not have understood the simple vulnerabilities exploited by the hackers well enough to ensure they were fixed. In Sony's case, it was reported the company faced a loss of $171 million the following year as a result of the breach.

All companies are a complex inter-connection of computer systems—doing a thorough risk assessment takes time and money. When you consider the size of a very large infrastructure like Sony's, the complexity of their organizational structure and their financial health, it's easy to understand why executives may not have spent what they should have on security. And when you then factor in the technical ease of some attacks, you can see why hackers continue to breach other organizations with little or no repercussions.

We were called in to Sony to patch up—literally—the vulnerabilities. We knew how the breach occurred, so we tested the systems to see which ones were still vulnerable, provided recommendations, re-tested them, and applied a remediation plan. Sony is actually lucky; many companies that can't afford to properly protect themselves simply don't.

Surprisingly, public tolerance has gone up—it's no longer shocking, but rather considered the norm when hackers breach giants like Sony or Equifax. There's a lethargy around the subject, and it's as if people already know that it's not a question of if, but when they'll be hacked. This then begs the question: why would you not protect yourself if you knew that someday your personal information will be breached?

Knowing that most online users, companies, and governments aren't properly protected, why wouldn't cyber criminals take full advantage and exploit every human error, software flaw, and website loophole? As the global online community continues to grow exponentially, and as people increase their attack surface with new Wi-Fi-enabled gadgets, hacking targets will only multiply.

Other reasons we're vulnerable

BIG DATA, THE "NEW OIL"

If you ever think cable, satellite, telecommunications, or utility providers have too much power, you'd be right. Cable, satellite, and telecommunications companies know what we watch, record, and download, while utilities companies know our credit history, how much water or gas we consume, as well as our payment history. But companies that collect AND store data in large quantities are scarier. Big data has become so valuable, it's sometimes called the "new oil." For example, banks monitor your transactions in real time and then offer products and services based on your behavior. (Or, from their perspective, they show that they understand your needs.) Have you ever received gold or platinum credit card offers over periods of continuous employment? Or, the opposite—credit card balance transfer offers to a short-term, low-interest card or line of credit? If you have, the bank simply made use of the data they have on you.

Equifax, TransUnion, Experian, Acxiom and thousands of data brokers also hoard and centralize large amounts of data (date of birth, social security number, driver's license, etc.) over the customer's lifetime. As the data grows over the individual's life, it can't possibly all be secured; the rate at which they acquire the data exceeds the speed at which new security protocols are implemented. So, if an organization like Equifax can't move fast enough to keep up, is it surprising that the May–June 2017 breach exposed the personal information of more than 140 million American customers?

If this doesn't scare you, then think about this: the five most valuable companies today—Apple, Amazon, Facebook,

Microsoft, and Google's parent company Alphabet are also scrambling to collect data every time you log onto their platforms. They're all fiercely competing to dominate and influence consumer technology. To make things even more interesting, their formerly your) information is stockpiled in huge data stores in the cloud. Is this a target-rich environment for hackers? Definitely.

THE MISUSE OF PRIVACY: WE'RE ALL BEING WATCHED

Privacy means nothing these days. The explosive growth of email, social media, and online marketing has made it impossible to roll back to a simpler time when we sent and received most of our correspondence by snail mail. People do not understand that they have given up their privacy when they post about their personal lives, and they do not know how their data can be used for ulterior purposes.

Early in my career, I was part of a social engineering assessment for a company in the Defense Industrial Base (DIB) industry. It was during the Iraq war, and Al-Qaeda was targeting company board members' children. Our job was to assess how easy would it be to breach a specific organization and to learn how susceptible the executives and their families were to kidnapping threats. We undertook an exercise to profile their executives. We used an open source application that allowed us to drill all the way down and learn about their children, tracking what they did on social networks, who they met, or where they might go on holiday. We quickly built their profiles and demonstrated how easy it would be for terrorists to access the children's profiles on the internet, threaten each of these families. The attack surface in the defense space was, and still is, highly attractive to terrorist organizations, so this assessment helped us determine if someone on the Internet could access their profiles, and eventually kidnap a family member to exact revenge.

Fast-forward to today. Governments around the world allow internet service providers to collect and sell the data of citizens and organizations, while websites and social media platforms track visitor activity. Everyone knows this. But most people don't know that the internet is not a safe place. They don't understand the concept of online privacy and security, and they certainly don't know that current security mechanisms aren't protecting them.

Even if you think you have nothing to hide, whatever you do online is never entirely private. There is no privacy online.

Lack of Internet Regulation

Most hacking skills are easy to acquire through a simple online search. With just a few clicks, you can find tools to download and use. Some are point-and-click, so you don't even have to learn how to code to attack your target.

Legally, there's minimal deterrence, even for a persistent hacker who has committed multiple breaches. Successful prosecution requires proving which physical jurisdiction the attack took place in, and that can be fruitless when trying to coordinate across geographical borders. If they bounce through a server in Japan and then to servers in Canada, the US, China, and Russia to finally hack someone in Canada, which country should prosecute? How many law agencies should be subpoenaed? Where is the jurisdictional boundary of the breach? How long would the process take? And at the end of it, how would they even know they have the right person? Law enforcement resources are too fragmented, and they don't have enough people sufficiently trained to conduct high-tech forensics. It would take too much time and resources. Most companies don't want to go to court and have all their dirty laundry aired, so they wouldn't prosecute.

Very few hackers get caught and are prosecuted. If I had to guess, I'd say only 10 to 20 percent of breaches are discovered and reported. Between the low barrier to entry via the free online tools and a lack of online regulation, a persistent hacker can rack up money and data undetected and repeat the process many times. When you add the defenselessness of most companies, even amateurs can break in and cause serious, lasting damage to an organization's reputation and bottom line.

The lack of online regulation, the ever-growing pool of big data, our own lethargy around privacy, and organizations' inability to treat cybersecurity as more than an afterthought are what make it so easy for "black hat" hackers to wreak so much havoc. What it means for you, aspiring cybersecurity specialist, is the opportunity to make a difference in educating the public against cyber criminals.

IMPACT OF CYBERCRIME, THE DAMAGES

The impact on everyday citizens includes identity theft, holding information as ransom, debit fraud, money theft, and unauthorized apps installed on their devices. Most victims have no idea how to defend themselves, and even fewer comprehend why they have become the targets. Cybercrime leaves an emotional toll on those who thought it could never happen to them.

In comparison, the impact on organizations varies depending on the industry they serve, the timing, and the duration of the breach. While losses can be monetary, they can also include fines if the organization doesn't comply with data protection legislation, a decrease in sales, denial of service to customers, loss of jobs, and operational disruptions that can cripple a business long after the breach. Here's a look at just a few of the biggest organizational data breaches to date.

- In 2004, a former AOL (America Online) software engineer steals 92 million screen names and email addresses and sells them to spammers who send up to 7 billion emails to unsuspecting customers.

- 2007: Hackers steal debit and credit card data of 45.7 million shoppers from nearly 2,500 T.J. Maxx and Marshalls stores.

- 2009: The US military erroneously sends back a defective unencrypted disk for repair, which holds records of 72 million veterans dating back to 1972, without destroying the data first.

- 2009: Hackers access Heartland Payment Systems' corporate and card processing network and expose 130 million credit card numbers; the hackers had first accessed the company's network two years earlier.

- 2012: Sixty-eight million addresses and encrypted passwords are leaked from Dropbox.

- 2013: Yahoo is breached and names, dates of birth, phone numbers, passwords, and security questions for 1 billion user accounts are compromised. The company discloses the breach in 2016.

- 2012: Adobe discovers that 38 million accounts were breached, including those of 33 million active users whose encrypted passwords were stolen.

- 2014: Hackers breach Yahoo's network and steal information from up to 5 million users; the company discloses the breach in 2016.

- 2016: The Democratic National Committee (DNC) is targeted by hackers believed to be engaged in political espionage.

- 2018 : Facebook Breach affecting nearly 50 million people, accounts were compromised when a vulnerability let hackers steal security tokens linked to their Facebook profiles.

Did you notice that the majority of these incidents were neither inside jobs, nor caused by human error, but malicious attacks?

Big companies aren't the only ones that are breached of course. However, despite the significant potential impact of the damage, businesses of all sizes and governments at every level continue to adopt a "wait and see" approach. Perhaps they hope they'll never be breached, or that if they are, the effects will be minimal and remain undetected.

Information is beautiful provides the best visualization of all the major breaches known to date (see next page).

It'll never be over

Cybersecurity is one of the fastest growing markets in information technology. Although viruses have been infecting computers for over thirty years, virus engineering has quickly shifted from sporadic vandalism to cybercrime. An exponentially increasing volume of malware (both sophisticated and crude) infects computer operating systems or crashes entire networks. It is sometimes hard to discover and can bypass known defenses.

There's no doubt that if we keep moving in the direction and at the speed we have been, we'll continue to be more connected and therefore, at greater risk. I've been involved in investigating and solving hundreds of security breaches, and I've seen it all first-hand: multiple systems online in different places, vulnerable infrastructures, tiny bugs that can develop into serious flaws, or networks that were already compromised.

http://www.informationisbeautiful.net/visualizations/worlds-biggest-data-breach-es-hacks/. Accessed 7 September 2018.

I sum it up in two words: "Shit happens!" Nothing surprises me anymore.

Meanwhile, hackers are growing increasingly more skilled and sophisticated, and they will adapt to infiltrate systems and get what they want, without a second thought to their victims. In our increasingly digitized world, the future is driven by data, and since everyone stores some type of data somewhere, everyone is fair game. And for aspiring "white hats" like you, it means having the opportunity to flex your technical, problem-solving, and communication skills. This means being one step ahead of the bad guys while staying cool under pressure.

Endnotes
1. This is the standard protocol for investigating an incident.
2. Penetration testing means trying to get access to an organization's systems from the outside.
3. SQL injection is a code injection technique used to attack data-driven applications, in which nefarious SQL statements are inserted into an entry field for execution (e.g. to dump the database contents to the attacker). For more details: https://en.wikipedia.org/wiki/SQL_injection.
4. An 'attack surface' is all the surfaces (physical, logical, human, process, technology) that are vulnerable to attack, and may be exposed to become targets.

2

THERE'S NO ONE WAY TO DO THIS

Chapter Summary

No two journeys into the cybersecurity profession are alike. It's also not a path that's easy to choose.

My curiosity of what's next has ultimately carved and progressed my career.

Culture dictates action. When you know which vulnerabilities are the easiest to penetrate and attack, you know where you can make the greatest impact. My first assignment in Saudi Arabia widened my eyes to how local cultural differences affect security and response procedures in different parts of the world. The attackers struck during Ramadan, a month-long sacred holiday, when religious customs are even more highly respected. What better time to have maximum impact?

We originally investigated from Houston, but a few days into it, we realized that the attackers might be on to us. Some 30,000 to 40,000 computers had their MBRs (Master Boot Record) deleted, which meant that they could not be booted up. Where there's little forensic evidence, it's harder to determine what happened in the environment. So, what we thought we could resolve remotely turned much bigger. Although Saudi embassies around the world were closed for the holiday, the country opened them especially to my team; we each drove or were escorted to our respective local country embassy, had our passports stamped, and boarded a plane into the country. For one of the team members they even sent a private jet to pick up their passport from their home. This was also a first!

It was an eye opener for me. After dealing with the geopolitics of traveling there and seeing the tension on the ground, we got to work. We quickly realized scale would be greater than we'd ever experienced. Normally when we're investigating, the company might be operating at 50 percent by the time we go in and there's some impact to their business operations. We're also usually able to create a boundary around the issue to contain it, so we can repair whatever has gone wrong in the environment. But in this case, the majority of the environment was destroyed, and the damage so widespread that there was little to contain.

We had to ensure that no other issues were left in the environment. Such a demanding and urgent recovery meant zero downtime in the client facility. We did nothing but work and sleep. The whole country was on holiday except us. It might sound negative, but it wasn't. In the end, the Saudis were great hosts, especially when they realized we were there to work and nothing more. We worked round the clock with them to help them recover and left them our hard drives on our way out. This is standard practice; nothing leaves the client environment or the country.

Most engagements I've worked on cross multiple time zones and geographical boundaries. It's necessary to be sensitive to, and aware of, the different cultural, social, organizational, and individual norms and behaviors that can impact the success of a project. And if you're earnest and want to succeed in cyber-security, I recommend having in spades a sense of humor and an open mind.

The testing side – understanding hackers

No two journeys into this profession are alike, especially in cybersecurity. Similar to my road to Saudi Arabia, mine wasn't a linear one; very few people wake up one morning and decide they're going into cybersecurity. It's also not a path that's easy to choose, and it's so obscure that most university students don't even know about it until they're in a computer science class and find it's an option.

Most professionals who started around the same time as I probably experienced a unique journey that led them to where they are today. I started in the industry during the dotcom boom when the internet was in its nascence. There was no career path to cybersecurity then; I simply stumbled into the field. At that time, I was working in the IT audit/security department of one of the big four accounting firms. Asking the same questions everyday—policy, operations, risk management—had me questioning what I was really doing there. I was bored. I needed to move—and fast.

I have been interested in computers from a young age. I always liked hacking and breaking into things, so I suppose I have a somewhat deviant mind. Things were quickly taking off on-line—businesses were going live, websites were cropping up everywhere, email was becoming a mode of communication for the masses, so I couldn't wait. "Online is the way it's going," I told my employer as I tried to persuade him to fund a master's course. It worked; they sponsored my two-year part-time Master of

Science in Information Security at Royal Holloway at the University in London, and this is where I received my formal cybersecurity education.

After graduation, I moved to ISS (Internet Security Systems), a very specialist information security team in Atlanta and worked in their X-Force team as a consultant. (Back then, accounting firms hadn't yet fully grasped the implications of cybersecurity nor understood the skillsets one needed to be in security, so going to a specialist company was the best thing I could do advance my career.) At ISS I honed my technical skills; ethically breaking into systems to test a company's security posture. This is also where I got my hands dirty and feet wet performing vulnerability assessments and penetration testing.

Next, I realized that I needed to manage security for an organization if I was ever going to become a well-rounded consultant, matching technical skills with strategic management ones. I left ISS and went on to further sharpen my technical skills at IBM, where they allowed me to run their ethical hacking team in Europe and to be responsible for the security of their larger client organizations as the CISO (Chief Information Security Officer). Companies, however, consistently paid little more than lip service to security, and I learnt in general that the CISO always became the patsy who got blamed, or worse, fired, for everything. Yet this experience gave me both insight and credibility on the management side of running security for large companies. It was now time to shift my focus again.

Around this time, I started researching and writing technical white papers and publishing them for the cybersecurity community. I also trained and taught aspects of cybersecurity through Royal Holloway and industry associations, and I started speaking at conferences and to various industry groups. I found through these speaking engagements that attendees wanted to know more about cybersecurity trends and prevention and what's really going on. It was sometimes shocking at times to learn how naïve the average individual is. But then again, my normal isn't their normal and my every day isn't theirs. Junior technical attendees and experienced managers from other fields would come up and ask me questions about how to enter the industry, which is how I came up with the idea for this book.

With breach incidents on the rise, I left IBM for Foundstone, which meant working for George Kurtz and Stu McClure, two internationally recognized cybersecurity experts. Foundstone was famous for many things, including the *Hacking Exposed* book series. Now owned by McAfee, Foundstone was one of those "Holy Grail" companies any aspiring cybersecurity specialist wanted to work for because of their focus on technical excellence. At Foundstone, I was quickly promoted to run the professional services division. Being a part of that team made me proud because it allowed me to fulfill a technical dream working with people of high technical caliber. It was like being part of a specialist team and going from the regular army to a special operations team, so I was happy to work with technical leaders in the space.

In the early days, internet security was more of an art than a science because it was about testing to see what might happen while *hoping* nothing would happen. Twenty years ago, when everybody was building e-commerce systems, there was very little testing done. People were just throwing together e-commerce websites and applications so they could be up and running as fast as possible. Security was just an after-thought, so customers would transact without it. Because no one knew about it except hackers, no formal penetration testing was done. It wasn't a science then— it was more an art because we didn't know what might happen. Since then, we've done a significant amount of testing in various environments and with different tools. The field has become more of a science because we now know what to expect out of certain tests and protocols.

At Foundstone, we hacked into systems to test their security, and we also helped companies perform incident response and forensics, which means helping them understand how the breaches happened in the first place. During that time, I became increasingly interested in forensics. While I had started in offensive mode— penetration testing—I realized that companies really didn't know what they were doing. While they knew breaches were an issue, they still had their head in the sand regarding cybersecurity because they typically only took care of the minimum requirements. I became frustrated at telling clients how to fix things, only to have them do some, or half of what I'd recommended. I'd come back later to do the next test, and they would say that they hadn't done any security upgrades. In between the two tests, they would have added new website functionalities, which only increased their vulnerability. "Secure by design" just wasn't a thought back then.

The general public also didn't understand the security implications of emailing or buying online or sharing their personal experiences on social media—that can all result in personal information being compromised. Online buyers believed everything was secure by default, while companies cared more about functionality and the aesthetic appeal of their website and applications than about making them secure—they didn't understand security. It was more about luring customers and making revenue than ensuring the customer's online activity was secure.

Things have obviously evolved since I started in the industry, but it's still irritating to see people and companies compromised for the stupidest things. For most companies, the marketing ethos is: get it done fast and make it look sexy. The push for rapid launches only exacerbates other mistakes, making those websites even more attractive to attackers.

Mistakes happen

Although I cut my teeth on penetration testing, I (along with most colleagues) made mistakes in the process. I remember that one of my teams was testing the security for a company that built and launched satellites—a very expensive product—and had scheduled a launch on a weekend. During the test, we caused an issue that forced them to abort the test launch. It was costly for that company, but a learning experience for us.

On another one of my early assignments, my team and I were asked to test a new financial system that transacted approximately $1.5 trillion a day. Because we had to test in a live environment, the client was paranoid about the downtime. As part of the hack, we managed to enumerate a list of all the users on the system, and we then started a dictionary attack against it to determine if they had weak or common passwords on the system. As luck would have it, the whole system went down in what we call a DoS (denial of service) attack. I had locked everyone out of their accounts because the client had implemented account lockouts after three attempts.

There I was in the server room typing away, oblivious to all. *Why is everybody running around like headless chickens?* I wondered, when all the while, I was the culprit. In my defense, I had previously asked the client lead if they had implemented such security measures, and he had said no; if they'd told me the truth, I wouldn't have tested this abuse case. In the end, that didn't matter—I had just stopped a system from transacting for about two and half hours. The client was pissed. It took thirty minutes to determine that it was actually an issue, another sixty to triage it, and then over an hour to give everybody their new accounts and reset their passwords and systems. It's not like switching a light on and off. I had proven the risk up front that the system was insecure and vulnerable to a DoS attack. But even scarier—I don't think the client saw it that way because he wasn't prepared for the real results.

Note that most penetration tests do not happen in a live environment. If you don't stay cool in these testing situations, things that shouldn't happen or that you least expect to happen actually might. Yet without that test, attackers can easily cause significant havoc that can later take even more significant resources to resolve. And when you do make a mistake, and proper quality assurance protocols have been followed, that's "okay" as long as you learn from it and don't make that same mistake twice.

The breach side – understanding clients

After breaking into multiple systems and seeing how easy it is to do so, you start to see certain patterns when you're defending. Using what I learned from penetration testing, I could see how I might break into a company or even a government entity to help cross-correlate the forensic evidence attackers left behind. This was new territory for me. I wanted to see what happens on the other side once a company is infiltrated. If I was going to help clients recover from breaches, I also needed to be able to run a security organization to understand how customers felt when I told them they were vulnerable. This is how I transitioned into Incident Response.

At Foundstone, my first major IR (Incident Response) engagement was with a strategic government think tank that called us with what they thought was a simple computer issue. Their servers kept rebooting when they applied Microsoft security patches. We found that a foreign nation-state had broken into their systems to access confidential research. Curiously, every time the researchers in the organization printed anything (emails, reports etc.) to their local printers on site, a duplicate document printed to another printer server in a foreign country. Innovative, I thought. So, we first had to determine what the problem was along with its context, the number of compromised user accounts, and any trace of malice left in the environment. Then, we made a containment plan to fix it all at once.

I left Foundstone to join a startup called FireEye which eventually acquired Mandiant, a company well known for its IR practice. We worked on a lot of IR cases and built an international team that, within two years, grew to over eighty people and now spans twenty countries.

From the first cyber-warfare in the commercial sector to Sony's breach and everything in between, I've been in the trenches as well as the boardroom. I've worked hard, learned a lot, and haven't been bored. My curiosity of what's next has ultimately carved and progressed my career. Alongside sharpening my technical skills, I also have developed my management style to select, build, and retain high-quality teams and handle clients. There are many books on theory and organization behavior; I won't bore you with the different types of management styles people use. I'll share what's worked for me.

My management ethos

I've honed my style of management working in mature organizations, major cybersecurity firms, startups, and smaller companies. The pool for cybersecurity experts is already quite small, and building a team of high-quality talents who are both intrinsically motivated and technically competent means I must tailor my leadership style to work with each of them. From my days at school till now, one of my core principles that underpins my management philosophy has always been to learn from, and apply the best qualities of, every person I work with.

Whether it's giving one-on-one constructive feedback (not "shaming and naming" in a group), rolling up my sleeves to jump in and get things done rather than ordering commands, having my consultants' backs and not throwing them under the bus in front of clients if something goes wrong, or reducing the amount of office politics, I try to acquire and use positive behavior and be a good example to others around me. It's all about the team and not the individual. We all have positive and negative qualities, and I've learned to focus on someone's best qualities and make sure each team member's strengths fills a gap and are congruent within the team.

The second core principle I try to instill in the managers I work with is that we work for the consultants and our employees. We don't work in a traditional pyramid where I'm the general who sits at the top and my underlings do everything I say. That's normally what you get in mature organizations where politics sometimes trumps employee well-being and development. Instead, I develop an inverse pyramid where I believe our job as the manager is to make sure consultants and employees have all the tools they need and that they're well looked after. When this type of setup is done well, it infuses loyalty and becomes part of the organization's mission and culture.

This leads me to my third core principle: I have a flat management style, with no hierarchy in the teams I build. There are no sacred cows or politicking like you might see in other industries. Anyone—from a first-year graduate to a brilliant expert—can walk in to my office and tell me I'm an idiot and I'm doing things wrong. Then, it's up to me to justify my reaction and my decision.

Cybersecurity moves in such a fast environment that I have to quickly assess what someone on the front line defending against attackers is saying before I make what must be a swift decision on how to proceed. A siloed management structure, or one with multiple barriers, doesn't work in our environment. An open communication channel can disseminate information to all the consultants so they can react quickly. This makes consultants feel safe to do their work or come to me with any issues. In cyber security, information is not power; it is an asset that must be shared, so I share everything unless it's something strategic or confidential. When we all communicate clearly and transparently, everyone should understand the decision-making process. We can, therefore, focus on our collective mission, whether it's facing the enemy and dealing with an attack or facing the client and ensuring we do a great job. Where there's transparent leadership, everyone can succeed.

Lastly, I believe that you shouldn't be afraid that people may be more intelligent than you. Someone on my team who is smarter than me doesn't diminish my value, but rather, makes them someone I can learn from. And I want to hire and learn from the best. So, I tell consultants and teams I lead to always try to hire people who are smarter than they are.

It's all about building high quality teams

This work requires nurturing and building teams and supporting them through their career progression. One of my core responsibilities is hiring and building teams where there aren't any. First, I find the talent—from referrals and networking—and recruit them to join me in my mission. Once they're hired, the fresh pool of talent needs to become melded into one team, one culture, one philosophy of thinking. It all gets done very quickly. Then, they're technically enabled to do their job, no matter where they live.

The majority of new hires work from their home country.

Recent college graduates are encouraged to visit the office environment, especially if they've had little corporate experience. New hires with at least five years of experience are more likely to start working remotely, but that depends in part on their maturity level. They must demonstrate their raw baseline talent before receiving the intensive methodology, tooling, and culture training that will enable them to work as one team from anywhere.

When you hire people from all over the world with different philosophies and from different educational systems, you sometimes have to break down cultural barriers so they can work together. If I hire someone in Australia and another in Norway, they have to be able to work cohesively while under pressure. Does managing different people in different time zones get challenging? Yes, it does. It's challenging, and someone always loses out. Either the Australians will lose out or the Norwegians will. And as the distance between a head office and the geographic location of a remote worker grows, the communication level dramatically degrades, and people from both remote locations will, at some point, feel cut off from the mothership. One of the keys to successfully managing a team is making yourself available to them.

My team-building methodology is usually structured, but because I'm in a fast-paced startup environment, something occasionally slips through the cracks. It's not like working for an IBM where there are multiple bodies, departments and a large pool of resources. When I'm switching hats between setting up teams, proving results, and training new hires, a lot of things happen at once.

Our current industry environment makes it fairly easy to find "a seat on the bus." If you're technically strong but don't have soft skills, you'll have an easier time than if you excel at soft skills but have little to no technical talent. If it's the latter, you'll still find a seat, but there will be fewer choices available. This is an important distinction to make because in a dream scenario, every team member is well-rounded and possesses all the skillsets, especially on the consulting side, which involves dealing directly with clients. Who wouldn't want everyone they hire to have strong technical skills, be great with clients, perform detailed quality assurances, be able to travel, and be available to work no matter the time zone? I know I would. But I've found in building teams that the junior members are highly technical and have less management and soft skills, so they need nurturing and training in those areas. It's also easier to build on their raw technical talent and train them into management roles than it is to turn those with strong soft skills into technical specialists.

IT'S ALL ABOUT CLIENT MANAGEMENT

The way I work with my clients typically hinges on the type of engagements I am contracted to provide (within consulting). Depending on the use case, whether the contract is for proactive testing or responding to a client breach, I have two different approaches to managing how clients react in each of these situations.

In proactive testing, we assess the client's problems and build a solution to address their needs. It's similar to one–on–one consulting where you need to further qualify and understand their issues, whether it's testing their website or network. From a strategic standpoint, I need to understand the client's situational awareness and environment (technology, structure, organization, politics), and craft a solution and an engagement that makes sense for them. To do this, I have to be transparent about what can and cannot be one while managing expectations, and fully explain the risks and possible downtime. Meanwhile, the client must be fully aware of the expectations and that, if mistakes do happen, we'll own them and work quickly to find a resolution.

Client dynamics differ in a response engagement based on where they are in the process. For example, if their systems are down for three days before they call us, it means we're walking into highly stressful conditions and we have to manage the client and their environment very carefully. We have to be ready to potentially tell the client, "You're doing this wrong," even if we ultimately do what they tell us to do despite our recommendation. In other situations, we must tell a client they're doing something the wrong way and give them the choice to either carry on without us or spend money with us to resolve things correctly. In such cases, we know they won't be successful, because we've seen so many other clients make the same mistakes.

And so, if they choose not to fix the issue, or choose to simply implement a partial solution that still leaves them vulnerable, we have to be prepared to leave money on the table and walk away.

Some clients respect our straight talk and see quickly that we care about what we do. Others choose their own path and carry on, but after running like a hamster on a wheel for another day or so and getting nowhere, they end up calling us back. Telling a client up-front what we can and cannot do is key to IR client management.

Managing client expectations is crucial to our success. Incident Response is much like the ER where a patient comes in asking how long it will take before they can go home, but doctors can't answer until they've run battery of tests before and after patching them up. The patient might know how initial signs of a heart attack, but the diagnosis later shows signs of kidney failure or a brain tumor. So, when we tell clients a fix will take days or months, they don't expect to get a final report immediately. And if attackers are still in the system while we're working in it— this happens often in nation-state cases—and they try to hide their tracks because they can see that we're already on to them, we let the client know what's going on.

3

DISCERNING A HACKER'S WORLD

Chapter Summary

It all comes down to one thing: it's easier to attack that it is to defend.

Today's hackers are sophisticated and detail orientated, using both simple and advanced technology to find and hit their targets.

When you better understand a black hat's motivation, you also better understand the risk and actions to take.

Sometimes it doesn't matter if you have implemented the best computer cybersecurity in an environment. If someone can walk into the room where the computer is located, they can physically take over that machine and all its data. While there are solutions to protect against such attacks, a lot of organizations have not implemented them for a variety of reasons. Security starts at the outermost layer: the physical security around the environment. Then it moves through the technology stack to the core. We call this the onion layer security model[1].

Securing the physical environment

Early in my career, I was part of a team contracted to test a global organization's security posture over a two-week period: this included its physical environment, people, and processes. There are different aspects to performing a security assessment (penetration testing/hacking). The premise is that if you can walk into a building and take confidential information, you don't need to hack in electronically. Companies are only as secure as their weakest link. You might be asked to find and take certain physical documents, access electronic files, or, as in this example, both. The confidential information we were tasked with obtaining related to research for a then-current public health scare.

Our first task required us to find out which company locations were involved in the research project. We used open source intelligence to identify all the organization's research facilities around the world, of which there were hundreds. We used social engineering techniques to narrow down to the two physical locations we needed to target. We then drove to the target locations, which were patrolled by an outsourced security organization with CCTV surveillance.

For the first location's physical test we assumed the persona of a printer maintenance engineer. The story was that we were there to fix some broken printers. Wearing the fake contractor badges we had made, we easily tailgated our way in and out of the "secure" facilities. Once inside, we looked for the physical information—files and folders on the activity—in the non-electronic world. We also installed a wireless access point into their network so that we could just sit in the parking lot, log into their network, and hack them from the security of our car.

At the second location, believe it or not, we stumbled upon the company's computer that creates photo IDs and access badges to all the physical areas in the organization. It was left logged on. Bonus. We used the machine to create for ourselves three permanent badges with 24/7 physical access to all areas for this organization. And how did we get inside to get those badges? We dressed up in our smartest suits and walked in through the side delivery entrance during the lunch hour rush. People were very polite and held the secure doors open for us to walk through. We then made ourselves comfortable around the break rooms and toilets until most of the staff had finished for the day. We started the next phase of our assignment, physically searching offices, as the cleaning crew began their night shift. And yes, we found the required documents with sensitive information about specific activities the company was engaged in.

Accessing physical paperwork can be incredibly easy, especially in companies that maintain a lot of paper documents. In some engagements, I've just walked into an office looking for a physical filing system, only to find the keys laying on the cabinet. If we can't find a key, one of my colleagues might have a lock-picking it, which is useful, since we don't want to damage anything. We find the requested files, take a picture or scan the documents, and put it back. In companies that operate in low-tech environments, we might find passwords jotted on a sticky note and stuck to an employee's computer screen. This is scary. What if a company is in the middle of litigation or sensitive commercial discussions or an employment tribunal? In such cases, the client might be using a code name for an unlaunched product or new software that, if discovered by an intruder, could become a goldmine for any hacker.

Executing any penetration tests are highly confidential, and only the client and a couple of their executives or legal team will be involved. Company staff will not be told. And so, if a security guard sensed something was off and asked me what I was up to, I would first try to talk my way out of it. If that failed and they still tried to take me in, I have what we call a "Get Out of Jail Free" letter supplied by the client. It has a phone number to one of the executives in the company who is aware that the penetration testing is taking place.

These types of attacks are getting easier as companies standardize their physical access control onto a couple of widely used systems. In these cases, you don't even need to find the badge creation system to create badges. Depending on the technology, you can clone an access card that allows you to swipe the reader and enter a building. But here's where high-tech building security goes wrong. We're increasingly connecting commercial building functions to the internet, including heating and cooling systems. Smart technology has helped organizations reduce their energy use, so that centralized setups in hospitals, universities, utilities companies, research facilities, or nuclear power grids worldwide can operate efficiently. But these same energy-efficient buildings are now much more vulnerable and attractive to hackers who want to control their management systems or shut them down. When you add different systems from different vendors across many buildings over time, it means that cybersecurity is deprioritized and not front of mind.

At the end of the day, nothing beats a physical attack or a phishing email—they are the simplest and least costly ways to access the required data. As we all know, phish attacks are one of the most effective attacks against employees of a company or an individual. The attack needs only one person in an organization of twenty thousand to click on the link to potentially compromise their machine and allow access to their account and passwords. And as more organizations take their physical environments online, the number of ways to attack and hack an organization increases.

Who are the Hackers

When it comes to hacking, there's the good, the bad, and everything in between. Long gone is the idea of a spotty teenager dressed in a black hoodie and hiding behind a computer screen in his parents' basement. Todays' hackers are sophisticated and detail-oriented, using both simple and advanced technology to find and hit their targets. They're not always after financial gain. They sometimes want recognition, or they want to make a political point, or they are simply attracted to the mental challenge. They have varied educational levels and backgrounds. They can also be part of a lucrative business with ample repeat business—if they're good enough not to get caught. Broadly speaking, hackers can be classified according to common threat actor categories.

Government sponsored: These attackers are highly capable and have their motivations (military, political, civil disruption, or propaganda) for acquiring and launching cyberattacks. Active state-sponsored groups are those you've no doubt heard of in the news, such as China, Iran, Israel, North Korea, Russia, and the U.S. Examples include Chinese-based APT16 that launched spearfishing campaigns against Japanese and Taiwanese organizations and APT28, a Russian group that reportedly compromised the Democratic National Committee in 2016[2].

Organized crime: These groups and networks are typically driven by profits and conduct attacks against citizens, businesses, governments, and critical infrastructures. Attacks against individuals are usually geared toward collecting Personally Identifiable Information (PII)—social security numbers, health records, credit cards, and banking information. Examples include financial crime group FIN5 which targets the restaurant, gaming, and hotel industries for PII information[3].

Hacktivists: These groups break into systems to expose what they feel is wrongdoing by an organization or government. They have a political agenda; they see themselves as social activists and aren't motivated by profit.

Insider threat: These are usually former, terminated, or disgruntled employees who want to exact revenge, make a statement, steal for a competitor or new employer, or for personal gain.

Opportunistic: Hackers (or "script kiddies") who want to garner attention or gain credibility in the hacker community.

In addition to the apparent differences between categories, it's important also to note the similarities that exist across the board.

First, hackers have no geographical or physical boundaries. They can work from anywhere, and this is part of the reason the best hackers are hard to catch.

Second, they start small and gradually learn more about programming, operating systems, and networks. Sooner or later, they realize that they must choose between making fast money by exploiting security flaws or choosing the good side—white hats.

Third, these career hackers are nimble and adapt quickly to new technologies and methodologies, which makes attribution more difficult. They're also relentless and resilient, and are happy to take on technical challenges, such as cloud computing, artificial intelligence, Software-as-a-Service, and encryption.

Typically, hackers who get caught are the low-level operators and at the bottom of the totem pole. Masterminds are not as easily caught.

Trends, tools, and tactics used in attacks

Cybersecurity isn't a top priority for most of us, yet cybercrimes are the third most expensive global illegal activity. The cost to businesses, individuals, and governments will continue to rise. The Center for Strategic and National Studies (CSIS) estimates that the global cost of cybercrime was between $345–$445 billion in 2014, or 0.62% of the world's GDP. In 2016, this was estimated to be around $445–$600 billion and 0.08% respectively.

What is driving this increase? According to CSIS, trends such as state-sponsored robbery, ransomware, cybercrime-as-a-service, anonymization services such as cryptocurrency, and personal information and intellectual property theft are the leading causes.

At the individual level, the Pew Research Center's "Americans and Cybersecurity January 2017" report suggests cybersecurity issues are related to user attitude:

- 64 percent of Americans reported at least one of seven types of data theft in 2016.

- Yet, almost half of them aren't confident in the federal government's ability to protect their personal information.

- 54 percent of online adults reported that they use potentially insecure public Wi-Fi networks, and about 20 percent of those use these networks to shop or bank.

What about countries? Who leads the world in international cybercrime? Nation-states are the most dangerous because they have deep budgets and are protected from law enforcement. Some nation-states even participate in financial cybercrime. For example, North Korea attacked at least three South Korean crypto-currency exchanges in 2017 alone. Between 2015 and 2016, the country also targeted SWIFT network banks in developing countries such as Bangladesh, Vietnam, and Ecuador.

On September 6th, 2018, the US Department of Justice formally charged a North Korean programmer for some of the biggest cyberattacks in recent years[4]. According to a 179-page DOJ indictment, the US believes that Park Jin Hyok, a 34-year-old North Korean, is one of the many individuals behind a long string of malware attacks and intrusions[5], such as:

- The WannaCry ransomware outbreak of 2017.

- Attempts of hacking US defense contractor Lockheed Martin in 2016.

- The 2016 Bangladesh Central Bank cyber-heist.

- The breach at Sony Pictures Entertainment in 2014.

- Breaches at US movie theatre chains AMC Theatres and Mammoth Screen in 2014.

- A long string of hacks on South Korean news media organizations, banks, and military entities across several years.

- Hacks of banks all over the world from 2015 through 2018.

The DOJ says Park was an active member of a government-sponsored hacking team known in the private cybersecurity sector as the Lazarus Group. But in reality, officials say, he was also a government employee working for a government-owned company named Chosun Expo Joint Venture.

Note that North Korea has said that a man charged with hacking Sony Pictures in 2014 is a "non-existent" individual and warned the US that its accusation could have a negative effect on relations between the two countries[6]. Can international law be enforced successfully against the reclusive nation? It would be a feat.

What else does this tell us? A lot of countries use the internet, and some are more advanced and sophisticated than others. However, being more advanced also means they are more vulnerable to any cyberattack because they aren't fully aware of all the potential consequences. In this case, everyone stands to lose.

When you better understand a black hat's motivation, you also better understand the risks and the actions to take. With this in mind, let's look at some of the common tools and tactics hackers use. (Note: this list is not exhaustive but looks to provide you with insights to attack methods typically employed by hackers.)

1. RANSOMWARE

Described as one of the fastest growing online crimes, ransomware is malware that infects computers and restricts access to files or entire devices by encrypting them. It's usually deployed through phishing emails that, when clicked on, install ransomware on your system. The hacker usually assigns a deadline for the target to pay the ransom, and if the deadline passes, the ransom doubles or the files are destroyed or permanently locked. But it wasn't always this advanced. The first documented case of ransomware was in 1989 when floppy disks were sent to AIDS researchers, inviting them to fill out a questionnaire that assessed an individual's risk of contracting the disease. The disk was really a malware program that demanded $189 to regain access to their computers.

Today, ransomware targets consumers and just about any industry that stores sensitive information—it doesn't discriminate—individuals, small business owners, CEOs, and even police departments have been affected. And to make things more interesting, savvy hackers now monetize ransomware through Ransomware-as-a-Service (RaaS) programs that allow authors of the program to make their code available on platforms for other cyber criminals to use and target. If the victims of the attack can't work out how to decrypt and get a key to the code, they can email or call a help desk, and just like in a call center, have someone walk them through the process. Threats are also becoming increasingly sophisticated as detection evasion and file encryption capabilities make malware easier to spread and pressure victims to pay the ransom.

According to Cybersecurity Ventures, ransomware is growing at a yearly rate of 350 percent, and its damage will have exceeded $5 billion in 2017, which is a significant spike from $325 million in 2015.

2. DENIAL OF SERVICE (DoS)

Denial-of-Service attacks occur when a website is so flooded with traffic that users can't access it. This attack can also be performed by a network of zombie computers coordinated to attack a website from multiple IP addresses in what is called a Distributed Denial-of-Service Attack (DDoS). These attacks over-load the website, slowing it down for legitimate users, and are used to punish adversaries or for extortion.

These attacks can also be hyper-focused, where black hats target networks, systems, or applications in an attempt to use up a website's network bandwidth, compromise or deplete a system's resources, or disrupt or consume significant applications with one goal: to cripple business or government operations by either slowing them down or crashing them.

In 2016, New World Hacking claimed responsibility in the DDoS attack against the BBC website. The self-proclaimed anti-ISIS group claimed to have been testing their server power when they took down the website for hours. What's equally as scary is that some of the perpetrators were rumored to be college students at the time of the attack.

3. APPLICATION AND INFRASTRUCTURE ATTACKS

These attacks target and infiltrate websites and servers to access confidential data within organizations or governments. They use basic techniques to easily circumvent the security devices everyone already knows about, including firewalls, antivirus products, etc. I recommend reading *Hacking Exposed* to understand these types of attacks in technical detail.

4. PHISHING

You're already familiar with random emails that look seemingly legitimate—from a company you already do business with, such as a bank, retailer, or software manufacturer—asking you to click on a link or download something. Hopefully, you haven't fallen for this trap. This malware will either infect your computer or take you to a website that looks legitimate, but it is a way for the hacker to capture your login credentials or other sensitive information.

Phishing (as in fishing for information) continues to be a threat, even though most of us are sophisticated enough to see the signs of a spoof email (fake customer/technical support email address, forged logo, modified email format, or URL). Part of the reason is because it's not limited to emails; a hacker can also try to access personal information by text, through social media, instant message, or a simple phone call.

Tax season is a prime time for phishing attacks of all types. Someone may impersonate an Internal Revenue employee and call a taxpayer about paying a fictitious debt or ask them to leave personal information on their voice mail. A fraudulent email might request information that doesn't normally appear on a tax return or that the revenue office already has on file. A recorded phone message could urge the taxpayer to log onto a website for more information about donating to a tax shelter scheme. Fraudsters are often aggressive; they threaten the individual with additional fees, jail time, or deportation if they don't comply.

5. BRUTE FORCE ATTACKS

In a brute force attack, the initiator attempts to crack a password or to try and find hidden website pages using automated software. The hacker tries combinations of letters and numbers to generate possible password sequences. In a reverse brute force attack, a hacker tries one password against multiple usernames. Depending on the type of system, brute forcing the password can take hours or longer as long as there are no limits to trials and the hacker doesn't get blocked.

White hat vs. black hat: Why choose the white hat?

In your whistlestop tour into my world, you've now gone beyond the basics of cybercrime and cybersecurity and know more than the average internet user. You know about the perks and rewards of cracking codes and infiltrating computers, networks, and applications, and scaring or coercing victims to do what you want. Morals aside, there's virtually no downside to black hat hacking if you don't get caught. It's access to easy money and possible fame. But, is black hatting all it's cracked up to be?

It takes a different form of morality to prey on people's fears and desires, and the risk is very high if you're caught. If you are convicted, you might have a hard time finding a legitimate job once you're released. If, by that time, you've moved on to something else, will it have been worth the negative exposure?

It all comes down to one thing: it's easier to attack than it is to defend. With free online tools, the willingness to learn, and some patience, one can easily become a hacker and exploit vulnerable systems because most companies and governments are in defense mode—they neglect taking care of the basics. Security patches, upgraded software, and strong passwords are an afterthought.

Meanwhile, individuals tend to rely on the government or someone else to protect their data. Remember that government think tank (from Chapter 2) that kept unintentionally sending documents to a printer in a foreign country? They still call me every year, and each time we have a conversation that goes something like this.

"Hey Bill, we've got a problem."

"I know what it is. Have you made any of the changes I suggested yet?"

"No."

"Okay, it'll cost $X to come and fix it."

Every time.

Believe it or not, for some companies, cybersecurity becomes political. They think it's too hard to do and will cause so much disruption that it's easier to apply a bandage over it and get back to business. The issue goes away for some time, but it always comes back, and when it does, I have to explain it to the executives all over again. It's like me telling them they have a cough, and I give them some cough syrup. But when the problem persists, other things begin to fall apart, and after I've gone as far as doing a CAT scan and told them they have terminal cancer or worse, they still only want the cough syrup. Sure, the cough goes away, but because they know they'll be coming back to me at some point to resolve the more significant issues, why not maintain the status quo?

At the same time, the more people become online users, the more the world continues to build complex computer systems, widening the attack surface. All of this makes it a no-brainer, as I said earlier, for a black hat to unleash significant damage to a system that was never designed for security in the first place. That's right: the Internet was designed for availability and resilience. Security was never part of the protocol.

As long as we continue to build integrated computer systems and exceed our capacity to secure these assets, there will always be someone out there who will try to exploit them. So, there should also be someone to help defend them. Hopefully, I've given you enough grounds to choose the right side. If not, let me give you even more reasons of why you should choose to be a white hat.

For the newcomers to the subject of cybersecurity I include two great graphics from the UK National Cyber Security Center to help you get up to speed.

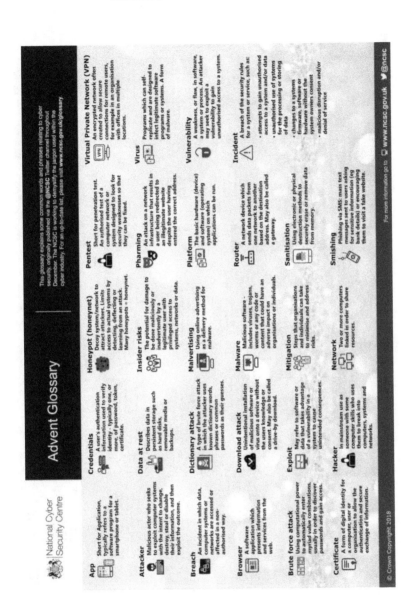

For more details go to Infographics at the NCSC (last updated 05 Jan 2018). https://www.ncsc.gov.uk/information/infographics-ncsc.

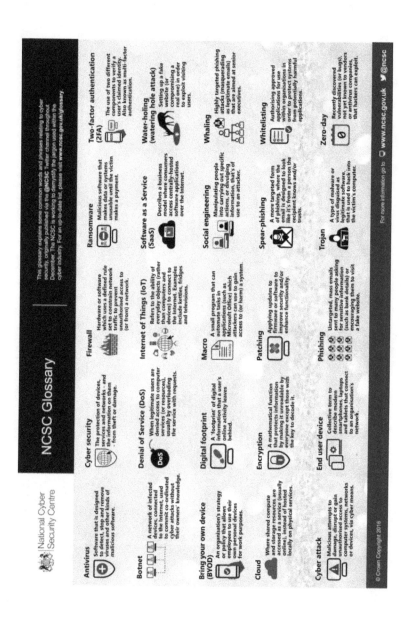

NCSC Glossary

This glossary explains some common words and phrases relating to cyber security, originally published via the @NCSC Twitter channel throughout December. The NCSC is working to demystify the jargon used within the cyber industry. For an up-to-date list, please visit www.ncsc.gov.uk/glossary

National Cyber Security Centre

Antivirus
Software that is designed to detect, stop and remove viruses and other kinds of malicious software.

Botnet
A network of infected devices, connected to the Internet, used to commit co-ordinated cyber attacks without their owners' knowledge.

Bring your own device (BYOD)
An organisation's strategy or policy that allows employees to use their own personal devices for work purposes.

Cloud
Where shared compute and storage resources are accessed as a service (usually online), instead of hosted locally on physical services.

Cyber attack
Malicious attempts to damage, disrupt or gain unauthorised access to computer systems, networks or devices, via cyber means.

Cyber security
The protection of devices, services and networks - and the information on them - from theft or damage.

Denial of Service (DoS)
When legitimate users are denied access to computer services (or resources), usually by overloading the service with requests.

Digital footprint
A 'footprint' of digital information that a user's online activity leaves behind.

Encryption
A mathematical function that protects information by making it unreadable by everyone except those with the key to decode it.

End user device
Collective term to describe modern smartphones, laptops and tablets that connect to an organisation's network.

Firewall
Hardware or software which uses a defined rule set to constrain network traffic to prevent unauthorised access to (or from) a network.

Internet of Things (IoT)
Refers to the ability of everyday objects (rather than computers and devices) to connect to the Internet. Examples include kettles, fridges and televisions.

Macro
A small program that can automate tasks in applications (such as Microsoft Office) which attackers can use to (or harm) a system.

Patching
Applying updates to firmware or software to improve security and/or enhance functionality.

Phishing
Untargeted, mass emails sent to many people asking for sensitive information (such as bank details) or encouraging them to visit a fake website.

Ransomware
Malicious software that makes data or systems unusable until the victim makes a payment.

Software as a Service (SaaS)
Describes a business model where consumers access centrally-hosted software applications over the Internet.

Social engineering
Manipulating people into carrying out specific actions, or divulging information, that's of use to an attacker.

Spear-phishing
A more targeted form of phishing, where the email is designed to look like it's from a person the recipient knows and/or trusts.

Trojan
A type of malware or virus disguised as legitimate software, that is used to hack into the victim's computer.

Two-factor authentication (2FA)
The use of two different components to verify a user's claimed identity. Also known as multi-factor authentication.

Water-holing (watering hole attack)
Setting up a fake website (or compromising a real one) in order to exploit visiting users.

Whaling
Highly targeted phishing attacks (masquerading as legitimate emails) that are aimed at senior executives.

Whitelisting
Authorising approved applications for use within organisations in order to protect systems from potentially harmful applications.

Zero-day
Recently discovered vulnerabilities (or bugs), not yet known to vendors or antivirus companies, that hackers can exploit.

For more information go to 🌐 www.ncsc.gov.uk 🐦 @ncsc

Endnotes
1 For more details on what is the onion layer security model https://securityintelli-gence.com/data-security-defense-in-depth-the-onion-approach-to-it-security/
2 https://attack.mitre.org/wiki/Groups
3 ditto
4 https://www-zdnet-com.cdn.ampproject.org/c/s/www.zdnet.com/google-amp/article/how-us-authorities-tracked-down-the-north-korean-hacker-behind-wanna-cry/
5 https://int.nyt.com/data/documenthelper/274-park-jin-hyo-com-plaint/7b40e5ed5b185f141e1a/optimized/full.pdf#page=1
6 https://www.bbc.com/news/world-asia-45522654

4

EVERYDAY CONSUMERS - THE UNSUSPECTING VICTIMS

Chapter Summary

Hackers are attracted to the proliferation of consumer data, the lack of Internet regulation and the complacent attention towards personal privacy.

We must take more individual responsibility for our online activity. It's up to us to protect ourselves and at least take care of the basics and have the attitude that everyone wants our data because everyone does.

Sometimes organizations are unaware that their systems have been compromised until their clients, everyday consumers, report to them unaccountable charges and/or transactions from their statements.

The weirdest client call I've had relating to a case like this came from a Russian bank at the time of the country's invasion of Ukraine. A hacker had compromised their ATM network using memory resident malware. Such an attack is very hard to detect. The infiltrator had already been stealing hundreds of millions of dollars from them, and the bank wanted us to help them with the forensic investigation. But that wasn't all.

"We know who's responsible," the client stated. "Our authorities caught him in Russia, but he managed to escape and is currently hiding in the Ukraine."

"Well, I'm not sure how I can help you."

He went on, "We know exactly where he is—in a compound. What we need you to do is trick him into leaving the compound and then put him on a plane and send him back to us."

I was stunned.

"We also know they've got armed guards by the door, so you have to be careful."

Armed guards? He was serious.

Needless to say, I didn't go ahead. I told him we'd be happy to investigate but no more. It definitely wasn't part of my job description. I recommended they contact the Federal Security Service of the Russian Federation (FSB) to do the rest. Things can get dirty for Incident Responders; we do a lot of things, but we don't do extra-ordinary renditions. It just isn't one of our service offerings.

Trends in online user behavior

Let me be clear and reiterate to all potential Incident Responders: we don't extradite or detain people as part of our role. But we do have to investigate internet user behavior as part of our engagements to help us better understand why people do what they do and fall prey to known, as well as lesser known, attacks. For example, many of us shop online regularly, or as a desperate, last-minute attempt to get something done. We pay mortgages, manage investments and retirement funds, and make plans for our twenty-year high school reunion from our smart phones. We even make life-changing decisions online and choose to put more trust in online retailers who monitor our activity than in the person we just met in the flesh on a blind date (caution applies). Here's what I mean:

- 58% of online shoppers state convenience as their top reason for shopping online over brick and mortar stores.
- 51% of Americans don't trust the government or social media sites to protect their data.
- Almost half of Americans surveyed feel their information is less secure today than it was five years ago.

- 39% use the same or similar passwords across online platforms.

- 41% have shared a password with a family member or friend.

What this tells us about user behavior online is that we don't take all the precautions we should. We leave ourselves exposed to identity theft and risk acquiring fraudulent charges and mortgages for the convenience. And, bizarrely, we place trust in online shops, but we don't trust institutions to protect our information. There's definitely something inconsistent in the way we behave when it comes to how we protect our personal information. Why is this?

First, many consumers aren't educated enough about the basics of online security.

Second, even for those who know what to do, they're often too lazy to use best practices or update their personal security.

Lastly, people generally don't think cybercrime could ever happen to them, so they carry on as if nothing will happen.

Unintended impact of organizational breaches on consumers

If white hats study how consumers behaves, black hats will be taking advantage of those situations at scale. Hackers are attracted to the proliferation of consumer data, the lack of internet regulation, and the complacent attention toward personal privacy, which present many opportunities for them to create chaos. In the event of a breach, it is harder to catch even an unskilled hacker when there is so little enforcement.

Banks, governments, and various institutions have more control and influence over the proliferation of consumer data and the lack of internet regulation. They need at least some data to do business and interact with customers. The challenge is the unknown repercussions of those breached organizations who do not properly fix their vulnerabilities and pass on the risks to their unknowing clients, the everyday consumer.

Equifax, a US credit-checking agency, is an example of a company that retains a certain amount of data on its customers and whose infiltrator still remains at large. Equifax's website was breached in the summer of 2017, and like most breaches of this size, the full impact wasn't known for some time. The company didn't disclose the breach to customers until September. First, they said that 143 million Americans' names and social security numbers had been targeted. Next, the company, in their attempt to manage the aftermath engaged instead in a series of blunders that has been documented online. As of March 2018, the company reported that 2.4 million Americans' partial driver's license information as stolen, and more information was stolen from Canadian and British customers. If you were affected by this breach, you've probably asked yourself if this is truly the end of it—and rightfully so. Credit companies store the type of data that follows you and can affect what you try to do in the future. What's worse is that an unsuspecting customer who isn't affected today might just find out in a most embarrassing way that they don't qualify for a mortgage next year, or that they've been compromised for life.

Disappearing online privacy

Individual users can vastly improve their online security if they just take the time to make some adjustments that will make them less attractive to hackers. One glaring example is social media. This isn't the part where I bash you over your use of social media platforms. We all have reasons for using it, including those of us who use it solely for business purposes. But let me ask you this: how many times have you announced on Facebook or Instagram where you were heading for a family vacation or tweeted your exact dinner location live? Twenty years ago, most of us were all too happy to go on vacation and have no contact with those who weren't invited. Today, we're eager to overshare with strangers where we are, what we eat, who we're with, and when we're coming home. This data is very useful for burglars on a spree.

Remember the story in Chapter 1 of the executives whose children were at risk of kidnapping by Al-Qaeda? Hackers don't discriminate, and they won't hesitate to blackmail a parent after they've stolen their child's information, knowing that a child can unknowingly share highly detailed personal information without their parents' knowledge.

A few years ago, I helped investigate the VTech database

breach, which leaked the personal information of over 11 million customers—adults and children. This type of breach (reportedly an SQL injection) meant that email passwords, images, chats between parents and their children, and other sensitive data could be exploited. The engagement lasted a couple of weeks, and they eventually arrested someone in the UK. This breach wasn't sophisticated at all, but it's the type that occurs every day because so many companies leave the door open and still never expect to be burgled. For security professionals like me, it was frustrating to watch a company go through yet another breach that could have been prevented.

For consumers, it's part of the risk we take when using modern devices. Being more cautious of what you share is just as important as how you connect to the internet via your device.

Maybe you occasionally access your personal email or banking app through an airport or coffee shop hotspot. Or maybe you've read a digital version of a book (perhaps this one) connected to an airport Wi-Fi. In either case, how do you know that a malicious Wi-Fi hotspot wasn't acting as a legitimate one? Most of us are guilty of at least one of these actions, and by now, you're aware of the potential consequences you might face if someone compromises your personal computer. I'm suggesting that the responsibility to do better falls on all of us. Waiting for the social media organizations to do something may be too late.

The Facebook–Cambridge Analytica data scandal is a prime

example of how social media was used for ulterior purposes instead of the intended research purposes. Cambridge Analytica reportedly harvested over 50 million Facebook user profiles, and some experts alleged they used the psychographic information gleaned from the users' activity to influence them, the voters, in the election. Over a two-day Congressional hearing, Facebook CEO Mark Zuckerberg answered questions about how the company shares and uses their data. Weeks later, the European Parliament grilled him about data privacy. Mark Zuckerberg publicly apologized for the breach of private data: "It was my mistake, and I'm sorry. I started Facebook, I run it, and I'm responsible for what happens here." If you watched the hearing, you may have been surprised at some of the questions asked by the Senate committee. They were basic, and it clearly demonstrated that many of the senators were not fully conversant with how social media or the internet works.

Could the data Cambridge Analytica reportedly accessed have influenced the elections? Or would the information be at all useful? We may never know if Facebook will make any changes to prevent third parties or threat actors from accessing user data in the future.

But one thing is clear. When those responsible for ensuring the privacy and security of citizens know so little about one of the world's largest social media sites or which questions they should have asked to get the information they needed during a United States Senate hearing, we should all be alarmed. If lawmakers can't speak up for us, who will?

I'll say one last thing about social media. If you're a multiple social media platform user, you should remember that nothing is free. When you use these platforms, anything you post can be stolen and reused without your permission or knowledge. You might be using their product, but in the end, any platform that advertises to you based on your activity means that you are the product.

What needs to change

I hope by now I've made it clear that cyberbreaches can happen to anyone, anywhere, anytime. So, how can we, as consumers, do better to change the trajectory and reduce the number of breaches?

It's clear that we must take more personal responsibility for our online activity. It's up to us to protect ourselves and at least take care of the basics and have the attitude that everyone wants our data—because everyone does. This requires more education and a willingness to be proactive and not reactive.

We must also do better as a society. We live in a world where so many are keen to show off their new shiny object on social media but forget that their privacy is disappearing every day. If you tracked your daily online activity closely, you would likely find a handful of bad habits that, if changed, would significantly protect your online footprint. Can you keep yourself from posting pictures of your protein breakfast shake or of your cute four-year old son covered in paint? Only you can answer that. Consider this: your followers will still be jealous if you post your tropical vacation pictures after you get home. You don't have to post them in real time and risk a chance that a bad actor will take advantage of you while you are traveling.

If you only remember once thing from this chapter, let it be that privacy on the internet is a myth.

How to better protect yourself

There's no point in preaching about the negligence of those around you if your personal devices are still at risk. And since you're interested in cybersecurity itself and convinced of the merits as a career, you might as well make changes in your immediate environment before you start telling others what to do. Here are a few steps recommended to help you boost our own online security and better protect your activity, if you're not already doing so.

1. Make sure each of your accounts uses a unique password and change these passwords every 90 days to prevent hackers from accessing multiple accounts with the same password. Consider using password vaults to protect multiple passwords.

2. At a minimum, protect your devices with the basic protection antivirus solutions. Remember to do the daily signature updates (if this is how your solution works) and scan your devices.

3. Update any outdated or unsupported operating systems and install automatic service packs to keep all security

patches up to date.

4. Don't use public Wi-Fi networks to make credit card purchases, pay bills, or access your social media accounts. (Or just don't use public Wi-Fi!)

5. Don't fall for hacker bait. Pirating content or surfing gaming websites hosted in foreign countries and accessing ontent from peer-2-peer websites and pornographic sites can invite unwanted attention from hackers.

6. Limit the number of apps you allow to access your Facebook, LinkedIn, Twitter, and Snapchat profiles.

7. Be careful about logging into websites using your Facebook or Twitter information—you might be giving them permission to use or sell your data.

8. Google yourself occasionally to see where your photo or online activity appears.

9. Don't fall for phishing scams. Don't click on every link you see, delete emails from banks or retailers where you've shopped but that look suspicious, and be wary of answering surveys and quizzes from senders you don't know.

10. Check the privacy policy on websites you buy from—they're not all created equal. Some will not allow you to opt out of sharing your data or delete your data when you close your account, or they may not notify you of changes to their policy.

For further information, the UK National Cyber Security Center also gives some good advice on password security.

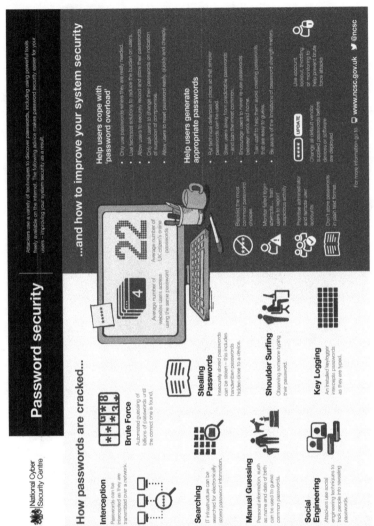

For more details go to Infographics at the NCSC (last updated 05 Jan 2018). https://www.ncsc.gov.uk/information/infographics-ncsc. Licensed under 3.0 of the Open Government License for public sector information. Compatible with the Creative Commons Attribution License 4.0 and the Open Data Commons Attribution License.

5

CYBERSECURITY IN ORGANIZATIONS AND GOVERNMENTS

Chapter Summary

The three key reasons why certain organizations struggle with implementing cybersecurity can be drilled down to cost, lack of visibility and complacency.

Our work as cybersecurity experts is to find where the vulnerable entry points might be to be in order to conduct targeted assessments of an organization's security layers.

Our work as cybersecurity experts is to find the vulnerable entry points to conduct targeted assessments of an organization's security layers, whether that's penetration testing, physical entry, or access via the internet. If a hacker can inject themselves into the supply chain of an organization (e.g., manufacturing process), steal something, or tamper with a production batch, they can seriously screw up the entire global operation of a company—before they've touched the technology stack. This is why we need to follow the onion layer model, starting at the physical security of a company before moving to the technology stack to the core. (See Chapter 3).

Some years ago, a global manufacturer asked my team to test the security of their product ordering system. Could we access the system, order a large quantity of products, have them configure the order and ship them? We secured the valid credentials by infiltrating and sniffing the network, got into the system, and ordered a highly customized $100,000 pink luxury mode of transport to be shipped to a specified location. This security breach relied on us first obtaining a user name and their login details to the system. It demonstrated that we could stop their process and put in some fake orders, or change the configuration of the models to a different color, and severely impact their business. It would cause a serious disruption to the supply chain and impact customer satisfaction. We found the vulnerabilities for the clients to fix.

Cybersecurity in business

Any company that uses the internet is vulnerable. Companies jeopardize their IT because they don't invest in adequate security measures, or even know what "adequate" entails. Even the simplest procedures like patching systems is basic-level hygiene that companies are responsible for, and not the government. This is the current landscape businesses are facing, according to the Identify Theft Resource Center (ITRC):

- Businesses accounted for nearly 51 percent of breaches in 2017, followed by banking, healthcare facilities, educational institutions, and government.

- Monetary damage to a large organization averaged $5 million, approximately $301 per employee.

- Nearly 70 percent of companies do not think antivirus protection can stop current threats.

Three key reasons why many organizations struggle with implementing cybersecurity can be drilled down to cost, lack of visibility, and complacency. (Note how similar they are to the reasons everyday consumers have security problems. See Chapter 4.)

Why are companies careless in protecting themselves? Perhaps they think any loss and fines associated with a breach, along with the investigation and remediation costs, will be so much lower than their total revenue that it's not worth their time to install and monitor modern security measures. The irony is that they've probably already been breached, and they just haven't discovered it yet. The possibility of lower sales, loss of customer loyalty, and destroyed reputation or brand equity isn't enough to deter them to make changes, so this attitude persists.

Because there is little coverage and visibility of the range of impacts resulting from hacking, too many companies naively believe they're secure by default. They are unable to understand the risks or believe criminals know how to exploit their vulnerabilities. Too many also operate with outdated systems and patches that, if updated, would keep hackers at bay. Part of the problem rests with the top layer in an organization, an older generation of executives who might know how to do business but don't understand technology, cyber or security. Therefore they don't fully understand how to protect their organizations. (Remember the Senate hearing with Facebook?) Until companies have board members with true technology and security expertise, new and adequate technology and security levels will trickle down too slowly.

To cap it all, while the reasons for hacking may be the same as ten years ago, the defenses against it aren't. The way we drive cars hasn't changed much since the first four-wheeled car was invented, however the technology we now use allows us to drive faster or use driverless, autonomous cars. The methodology behind computer hacking hasn't changed; its technology and methods have. Neither individuals nor companies have significantly raised their defense game, so hackers haven't had to change their attack methodology. I compare it to living in a castle while war rages around it. From a window, you see soldiers approaching on the horizon, and soon they're at the doors, beating them loudly. You focus on the window only.

Meanwhile, you've left the back door to the castle open to attackers. Except they're also tunneling from below ground and you can't see that the perpetrators are already inside. In the end, the attackers don't have to change their game much to get inside the castle. That's what I mean by lack of visibility, and this is what the internet is like every day. Physical and virtual walls may seem adequate, but attackers are always looking for a way in. Businesses and governments usually don't know that what they have isn't enough. That's why so many rely on outdated antivirus protection or a system patch for protection.

We're now well past the internet boom, so for companies to say they don't understand cybersecurity is, in my opinion, not defensible. This attitude might have worked in 2005, when the number of internet users worldwide according to Statista was a bit over one billion. The number of users has topped 3.5 billion. Cyber-hygiene is the one thing organizations can control but simply don't want to. They're unconcerned about taking care of the basics and don't want to admit it. If the majority of the non-executives sitting on the board are ignorant of the latest cybersecurity practices, and don't believe that they might be breached, and if simple things like patches aren't done, it leaves their organizations wide open to breaches. Cybersecurity, like finance, should be on the board's agenda at every meeting. Countless online resources, free and paid, can help commercial infrastructure developers cover the basics of cybersecurity and beyond, so for organizations to claim they don't understand the everyday risks and instead pay lip service to them is both lazy and negligent.

Companies demonstrate these lackadaisical attitudes when, in an attempt to avoid negative publicity, they don't admit to a breach. Attempting to control the narrative is understandable, given the long-reaching consequences that can ensue once the media gets a hold of a negative story. I'll discuss this later. But it can also backfire.

For example, Uber waited a year to admit that 57 million personal records, including email addresses, mobile phone numbers, and driver's license information, were stolen. For many, this attempt to ease the public, customers, and potential clients was misleading and too late for a company that was already struggling with rumors of being a hostile environment for female employees. Their new security chief, the highly credentialed Matt Olsen, said this "For any large organization, whether you're talking N.S.A. or a company like Uber, having a plan and having practiced and exercised how to respond to a breach is critically important," he said. Let's hope they do more than just prepare to "respond" to a breach.

Just as we saw in online consumer behavior, the human element impacts how businesses become vulnerable to cybercrime and how they defend themselves. As long as corporate system users perpetuate a casual attitude toward cyber risks and don't invest in prevention or even see what could harm them, even a novice hacker will find his way to confidential or proprietary information.

WHEN PRIVATE LIVES ARE EXPOSED: ASHLEY MADISON

Case in point. The most embarrassing of incidents can occur when someone's private online activity reveals unsavory activities. In the summer of 2015, Avid Life Media received a warning message from a group calling themselves the Impact Team ordering them to shut down their Ashley Madison and Established Men websites within thirty days or their client information would be leaked. As the deadline passed and the company struggled to contain the damage and solve the breach, the hackers reportedly published a torrent file containing company information (including the CEO's email addresses), email addresses, and mailing addresses of account holders—some of whom were public officials—along with partial credit card numbers and sexual preferences. The leaks continued as the hackers released user IP addresses, sign-up dates, state-by -state user lists, and even amounts spent on the company's services. Meanwhile, copycat hackers moved in to further scam compromised users into paying them to delete their files or threaten to send them to relatives. The mess seemed to have no end in sight. As users scrambled to find out whether their information had been compromised, for others, it was too late—in less than two months, the media reported two suicides associated with the leak.

The lesson here isn't about whether or not you should use dating websites. It's that all types of organizations are at risk, and this case represents any website in any industry. Users put themselves and possibly their loved ones in danger when they engage in high risk websites that aren't doing all they can to protect their users. According to individuals who were part of the anonymous Impact Team, the company's security level was bad. "No one was watching," so they used their technical advantage to unleash a world of hurt. And according to researchers CynoSure Prime, who reportedly cracked 2.5 million of the website's passwords in hours, the top ten Ashley Madison passwords included "123456," "DEFAULT," and "password." Not so smart for people who didn't want to get caught cheating. I guess the second lesson is if you're going to engage in this type of activity, just don't use 123456 in any form as your password.

How safe is your bank?

Banks are one of the top five industries highly attractive to hackers. Technology has brought us a long way from traditional banking practices that entailed waiting in long lines to speak to a teller and signing on the dotted line for every transaction. Credit cards, ATMs, mobile banking apps, and fintech companies are revolutionizing the way we bank. Although this sector spends considerable amounts to protect itself:

- According to the Identity Theft Resource Center, there were 69 breaches in the banking/credit/financial industry in 2017, believed to have exposed 2,781,270 banking records.

- A Security Scorecard survey reports 50,803 malware incidents in the 2,924 financial institutions they scanned between March 2017 and August 2107, with 45 percent of the banks having had at least one malware event in that same period.

- If you can't quite wrap your head around these numbers, here's another example. The 2016 Bangladesh Central Bank cyber-heist remains one of the biggest and most highly sophisticated attacks. Hackers managed to siphon a whopping $101 million from the bank's Federal Reserve Bank of New York account and split the loot between bank accounts in Sri Lanka and the Philippines. They had planned to steal $1B in thirty-five transactions, but only five transactions were approved.

POS and ATMs

To encourage spending, banks and fintech companies have made it even more convenient for consumers to buy. If you grew up in the 80s, you might remember that banking theft was mainly isolated to a stolen credit or debit card; you would just go to the bank, cancel the card, and replace it. Today, point-of-sale (POS) systems that allow you to swipe your debit or credit card to pay can also be compromised. It may not be the database but the system processing these transactions that gets compromised.

So, let's say that you went out today and ran some errands. You stopped by Whole Foods and at Verizon for a new phone. Then you capped off the day at your favorite coffee shop for a snack. The following month, you're horrified to see multiple debit transactions from multiple retailers you've never even shopped at. So, where was the compromise? The brick and mortar retailers? The coffee shop? Your bank? Or the ATM you used two months before? There are so many attack surfaces it is difficult to pinpoint where the compromise happened.

Hackers can also skim magnetic stripes at ATMs by placing devices over the card insert slot. They can see your pin through a pinhole camera (which they install) in the ATM. At the end of the night they have the data to create a fresh batch of credit/debit cards. Then, they go on spending sprees in foreign countries because the systems aren't interlinked, so by the time the fraud is triggered, they've already taken a million dollars off some five hundred cards.

While banks have certain detection systems in place, fraudulent transactions happen all the time. Using debit cards is crazy because they offer very little protection for consumers. And as in other industries, some banks prefer to absorb the loss, as there is a point of finite return in protecting the card data versus the amount of money that has been stolen.

So, are today's banking practices safe? Financial institutions have a duty of care to protect the systems you use, so they must protect your data and transactions. Meanwhile, as a customer, you should be using best practices, and if you see your bank not doing this as well, consider changing banks—sometimes easier said than done. To reduce my risk, I use a separate computer for financial/sensitive transactions and another for day-to-day activity.

For more steps to better protect your banking activity, review the checklist at the end of Chapter 4.

Ransomware and why companies pay for recovery

Businesses across all industries and affected centers are often subject to these ransom demands. Their reasons for paying, while always rooted in business recovery, vary according to the potential damages. One of the fastest growing online crimes (see Chapter 3), ransomware is impacting the business operations of organizations around the world, targeting individuals and organizations alike. In one case I worked on, a particular manufacturing company was hit, and all the data used for running the business was rendered useless as it was all encrypted. They couldn't even use email or access their ordering system. The attackers wanted $5 million in exchange for the key to their files, and we managed to negotiate it down to $800,000. They made the payment, recovered their data, and all was well again.

Along with access recovery, companies can have other reasons for not confronting hackers head-on:

1. There's a deadline, and they want to avoid a recovery fee hike.

2. It is cheaper to pay the ransom than investigate how the infection happened in the first place.

3. They want to prevent the incident from leaking to the press.

4. They don't want to report the breach to authorities, who will implement fees and penalties.

Ransomware is a great business model for attackers; companies reward their bad behavior with a payment, while there's no guarantee they'll even release the stolen data. It's also highly lucrative. Of fifty companies exploited, if only five paid $500,000, that's $2.5 million. All you'd need is the right skills and some patience to pull it off. And if you're extra lucky, the company won't even make the required changes to their infrastructure, and you can hit them again.

The healthcare sector—a deadly target

In May 2017, the National Health Service in England (NHS) was hit in ransomware attack known as WannaCry, which infected over 230,000 computers in more than 150 countries. The attack caused disruptions, canceling patient appointments and operations, and could have had much more serious impact on NHS's service to its patients.

As you can imagine, there are several issues around the privacy of patient data that go beyond connecting ailments to patients. Let's start with the availability of medication and supplies. What if you could stockpile all of the insulin, asthma pumps, or self-injectable epinephrine? Or, what if there was a denial-of-service attack and CAT scans or MRI machines were under attack? What if you could hack a hospital's wireless network and stop medical devices such as chemo pumps or dialysis machines from operating and used them to do harm to someone?

Thankfully, NHS's attack was resolved in the same day, but according to a report by the UK's National Audit Office, the organization could've prevented it with simple steps because they had been warned the year before that an incident could happen.

The role of the press

In 2016 we worked on the biggest bank robbery in the world. The Bank of Bangladesh heist[1] was uniquely challenging for two reasons. First, because it is a developing country, the logistics surrounding communications and traveling independently was very hard for the team when they worked onsite. Second, corporate governance was nonexistent—every time the team provided an internal report to the client, parts of that same report would suddenly appear in the press. In essence, all the information about what we were doing leaked like a sieve while we were trying not to tip off the hackers.

What goes on in the background during an investigation affects how breaches are perceived by the public and how they react. Companies normally call in forensics when they discover they have an issue. By this time, the narrative is already out and owned by the press, so we white hats are behind the curve when we arrive on the site. The client knows that they need to regain control of the messaging, so they start by putting a backstop behind the story to stop the bleeding. Companies normally release a positioning statement that acknowledges the issue and says that an investigation is underway. They don't want to admit any liability, nor how big the issue is, so after their legal team approves the language in the statement and everyone else agrees, the statement they push will depend on how much risk they want to take. It takes time for forensics to triage, so this gives us all some breathing room to hold the wolves, the press, and everyone else's opinions at bay.

We then investigate; what we're able to see depends on the evidence we found. For example, if a client routinely doesn't collect their logs or monitor security events, we only report on the facts evidenced in this environment. This is standard in a basic investigation. We should be able to tell the client what's happening in their system in a short period of time. We then feed that information to the client's incident team, which is usually made up of PR, legal, and part of the C-suite.

This is what typically goes on during an investigation. The savvy companies will have a process in place so that their PR team can stop the bleeding early. Companies that don't have a sophisticated messaging mechanism in place get bitten by the press. In the end, the press will always find something to talk about, and they will speculate and assume and are, therefore, very seldom correct. Few press outlets cover security breach stories accurately. This is because the press typically doesn't have the full details or context around an attack, but rather, bits of data they rely on. It's similar to watching the news coverage of any news event such as a terrorist attack. Everyone speculates on what's going on, including experts or a random person who was once in the army and has an opinion. But here's the thing: it's just an opinion, and they have no idea what's really going on behind the scenes.

I believe that the press in the Western world only knows and reports on 10 percent of breaches that are happening at any time. And where there is no free press, no one knows what's going on. I've worked a lot in countries where big breaches have happened, but nothing is shared with the public because the authorities can easily shut down the media. For a company to weather the storm and minimize the negative narrative, it should orchestrate things to keep their name in the press for as short a time as possible and take the biggest hit of exposure in the beginning.

When I look back at press reports on the Saudi breach I discussed in Chapter 1, I'd say that 80 percent of the reporting during the time of the event was way off, mainly because they weren't fighting the fight and seeing what we were seeing. The next time you see a report about a major breach, know that much of the reporting is the result of the children's game known as "telephone" or "Chinese whispers."

Behavior in government

I've worked across the globe to block intruders and to protect computer systems, networks, databases, and hardware, and it's always eye-opening to see how nations deal with and protect themselves from cyber threats. I am surprised at the lack of sophistication or maturity of governments employ to protect their citizens. I've found that the offensive capabilities of various countries are part of an unspoken "Best, Better, Worst" ranking system. For example, in terms of nation-states, the Chinese, US, and Russians are considered to be very sophisticated and very capable in performing offensive cyber operations. Also, although the majority of governments say they don't do them, they all do. They perform both offensive and defensive operations. When you examine just the defensive protections—the protectors of home nations—their maturity levels differ by country, as does their own citizens belief about the protection in place.

It sometimes surprises me that some countries aren't even at a basic level of offensive/defensive capability. And if you think the US is near the top of these capabilities, consider that even they have struggled unsuccessfully to protect their own sensitive data. In the end, all governments have been breached at some point—

disclosure depends on whether or not there's freedom of press in a country and how often they want to play the national security card.

Two prominent but separate breaches occurred at the Office of Personnel Management[2] (OPM). In one, personnel information of 4.2 million current and former federal government employees with security clearances was stolen. The personal information, including criminal histories of 21.5 million employees and contractors, was taken in the other. There's no telling the damage the hackers could cause with this amount of personally identifiable information. For more examples of US government data breaches, check out the list in the Appendix.

WHAT IS THE GOVERNMENT'S ROLE?

Who is responsible for protecting citizens and organizations from cybercrime? While the government has a say in how much of our information they need to do their job, we're still responsible for our own internet activity.

It wasn't always like this. Governments weren't originally responsible or anything. Critical national infrastructure is becoming part of the fabric of the internet, it became obvious that they needed to protect critical national infrastructure items. But the security standards were set at minimum levels, which makes it easy for intruders to hack their way in. Government agencies store more data than the private sector and often do so on antiquated and vulnerable systems. Governments are now trying to upgrade security protections, but individuals and organizations still need to provide their own security. For current insights on what the government's role should be, make sure to read the interviews in Chapter 7, particularly those of Patrick Olsen, Robert Coles, and Ramses de Beer.

Should we trust the government? In the end, although everyone is fair game including the government, that same government can also hack into whatever they see fit. For example, the US government has full access to anything it wants— all it needs to do is submit a Foreign Intelligence Surveillance Act (FISA) warrant to be let loose on your Gmail account. This shouldn't surprise you; governments have always spied on their own citizens and other countries for the sake of national security, and intelligence communities have ways of stealing things that you and I will never know about.

Another argument for holding governments accountable is that citizens never truly know what their own governments are doing. You don't need to look further than the possible Russian involvement in the 2016 US elections as an example of how quickly an investigation can become entangled and messy. But was Russia really involved? I think certain people within the intelligence communities know for sure—everyone else is purely surmising. And even if they uncovered solid evidence of interference, no one knows the potential repercussions. We may never know the truth.

Lastly, committees in government departments all rely on other people to tell them what's wrong. This means there is sometimes considerable papering over the truth about what's really going or of the current state of the health of the organization. Those at the operations level don't want to filter the bad news up and think they have control of it. They also rely on audit committees—run by accountants who know nothing about security—to tell them that everything is good. In the end, the top tier operates on a false sense of security (sounds like a Hans Christian Anderson tale of "The Emperor's New Clothes").

Here's the bottom line: All governments have certain standards and guidelines in place, but individuals and organizations should also be vigilant in protecting their own data. Even when regulations are established, no one should assume that they have closed all possible doors that can mitigate the risks.

What needs to change

It's clear that organizations and government agencies can do more to protect their customers and citizens. Most of them simply haven't covered the basics and continue to operate in an insecure manner, allowing hackers to access their environments without being detected. Check out what other industry experts have to say in Chapter 7. Lots of governments around the world do provide practical guidance for companies large and small. I also include infographics from the UK National Cyber Security Center as well as adding my own top suggestions at the end.

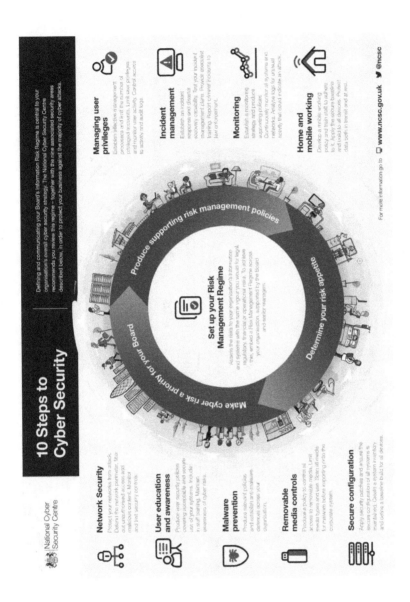

For more details go to Infographics at the NCSC (last updated 05 Jan 2018). https://www.ncsc.gov.uk/information/infographics-ncsc.

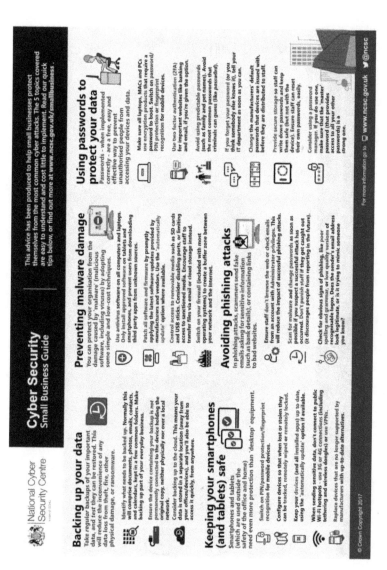

Licensed under 3.0 of the Open Government License for public sector information. Compatible with the Creative Commons Attribution License 4.0 and the Open Data

My top suggestions for organizations and governments:

1. All organizations need to take threat risks more seriously and understand how to protect themselves. Many of them think that auditing/compliance is security, believing that a control review is enough, but compliance only means they're following a command. It doesn't equal security.

2. All types of organizations should take a risk assessment to review their current security, identify their assets and possible threats, and create a cybersecurity policy.

3. They should be aware of their government's cyber initiatives and programs and get involved, in whatever capacity they can, in improving standards within their industry.

4. All staff need better training to know how to detect suspected malicious activity on computers and networks.

5. Access should be limited to only those who need it and staff who have high-level access should be monitored.

6. All types of organizations should be ready with a breach response plan.

Endnotes
1. Asia Wired - Bangladesh Cyber Bank Heist -https://www.youtube.com/watch?v=QLRA2HPRmGU
2. The OPM is where anybody that needs a security clearance is vetted.

6

INSIDE THE WHITE HAT WORLD

Chapter Summary

The fact that humans are always the weakest link is what makes cybersecurity experts valuable.

With such high demand AND a limited pool of qualified candidates, cybersecurity today almost guarantees that you can work from virtually anywhere, in any sector, and have job security.

A cyber expert has many roles, from being a pseudo-actor, conducting physical break-ins to tapping away at a keyboard for a penetration test or a forensic investigation. Aspiring white hats will find something within the spectrum to fit your skills, and pathways to establish your career.

I'd like to share a few more case studies that start to illustrate the technical and investigative nature of the job: are you curious?

CASE STUDY 1 – HOW EASY IS IT TO LOSE CREDIT CARDS?

We were asked to investigate a breach in a large bank who had just detected they had large amounts of data leaving their network. They didn't know what had been taken, how it had been taken, or who had taken it.

We flew into the country where the banking entity was impacted. Our technical investigation found that it was a very sophisticated attack; the time from launching the attack to exfiltration of the data out of the environment was approximately 12 minutes. There was little or no evidence of how the attack happened as the attackers cleaned up after themselves. As a result, we had to use advanced forensic techniques including "carving" data from memory to determine that the details of 8M credit cards had been stolen from the environment using an advanced SQLi attack.

Not atypical in such situations from a political client management point of view. I was pressured to stretch the truth on our findings to stop a trigger which would require reporting the breach to regulatory authorities in country. Needless to say I stood my ground.

CASE STUDY 2 – HOW UNSOPHISTICATED ATTACKS ARE AFFECTING INDIVIDUALS AND COMPANIES

A common attack involves standing data, such as back account details for a company's suppliers. The next time the company pays the supplier by bank transfer/ACH the payment goes to the attacker's account, not the supplier.

One company we worked with became aware of this when a supplier called to chase down an outstanding payment of $3M. Our forensic investigation included:

- Identifying the user account that changed the bank details.

- Analyzing a laptop for evidence of compromise. We determined that a spear phishing attack had been the vector of the initial attack with a backdoor dropped on that laptop soon after.

Variations of this attack have also impacted property transactions. Here the attackers compromise law firms or title companies that transfer funds from buyer to the seller.

CASE STUDY 3 – ADVANCED NATION STATE ATTACKS

My colleagues and I have documented a sophisticated attack named "SYNful Knock" where advanced threat-actors have deployed persistent malware that allows an attacker to compromise and gain control of certain models of Cisco Routers using a modified Cisco IOS Software image. The malware has multiple modules that are enabled via the HTTP protocol (not HTTPS) and controlled by crafted TCP packets sent to the device[1] (see Appendix).

The skills challenge

By now, you're more aware of the challenges individuals, businesses, and governments face in fighting against cybercrime. Additionally, hiring cybersecurity specialists is a challenge in itself:

1. The demand for skilled candidates outstrips supply.

    - The workforce gap was estimated at 1 million people in 2014: that's 1 million more roles than qualified people available. One industry report estimates the workforce gap will reach 1.8 million by 2022; another report estimates an even wider gap of 3.5 million in 2021.

2. Finding and hiring cybersecurity talent is hard.

    - It takes six months or more for 32 percent of enterprises to recruit for a cybersecurity position.

    - One in five organizations gets less than five applications, and only 13 percent get twenty or more applications for a cybersecurity posting.

It's clear that cybersecurity is a field with virtually zero percent unemployment, which makes it highly attractive to those who have the required skills. It should also be noted that this workforce doesn't suffer from the age stigma that plagues other fields. Age isn't generally factor, but you need to understand how fast the market is changing. It's your responsibility to make sure you understand the new technology and keep up with the times and maintain or improve your technical skills. And if your goal is to be in management or serve as the Chief Information Security Officer (CISO), you obviously need management experience too. As long as you have a good understanding of the technology, you don't have to be so hands-on. It's not as cutthroat as other fields because there aren't enough candidates to fill the gaps in the first place.

So, why is there such a disconnect between demand and supply, especially given the increasing threat landscape? First, the lack of education targeted to those seeking a career in cybersecurity means not enough young students know about the field. Students who take computer technology courses don't necessarily know about the different specializations such as artificial intelligence (AI), information management and analytics, bio computation, mobile computing or, you guessed it, computer and network security. So the problem begins early.

It unfortunately also persists across genders. A 2017 study by Frost Sullivan found that 69 percent of women hadn't pursued a career in information technology because they weren't aware of science, technology, engineering, and mathematics (STEM) opportunities. In a survey conducted by Kapersky Lab, 45 percent of women cross France, Germany, Israel, Italy, the Netherlands, Spain, the UK, and the US stated they didn't know enough about cybersecurity careers to have an interest in them.

But even when there's some level of awareness as part of formal education programs, the number of STEM graduates is still lower, and some sources say, plummeting compared to other disciplines. University systems are designed to train students to enter the workforce. In marketing, for example, there might be thousands of marketing graduates for ten jobs—it's a very mature industry. Or if you want to be an accountant, they create a funnel to prepare one hundred accountants, so that by the end of the year they can pick fifty of them. These are examples of well-defined markets. At the moment, there isn't a defined market for cyber-security people. In software development, coding, and computer sciences, while there is a funnel into those specific branches, the graduate pool is very small compared to the demand. There aren't nearly enough qualified candidates to fill the workforce gap.

Certain barriers also affect supply and demand. Most STEM graduates are men, which means that women are poorly represented in a male-dominated workforce. Today, women make up only 11 percent of the global cybersecurity workforce—a number that hasn't budged since 2013—even when they reported a higher level of education than men. The number is extremely low, considering that women alone make up almost 50 percent of the workforce in the US.

There are initiatives, however, that are working to change the landscape and correct gender imbalance. In June 2017, the Girl Scouts of America created eighteen cybersecurity badges to introduce Girl Scouts as young as five years old to cybersecurity information and deepen their understanding of STEM opportunities. And following Black Panther's box office success, Disney recently donated $1 million to help the Boys and Girls Club to fund their latest STEM program initiative. Make sure to check the Appendix at the end of the book for a list of associations for women in cybersecurity.

Visible minorities and individuals with disabilities are also under-represented in the cybersecurity workforce, even though the former make up 40 percent of the U.S. population.

What does this all mean? In the end, there's plenty of room at the table for many more cybersecurity experts, since there aren't enough people with enough skillsets to protect any one country's critical national infrastructure.

Which path to take?

When I started on this road, there was no typical path to cybersecurity, simply because there just wasn't a career path. If you were a computer science student, you might have learned about the industry close to graduation, or after you had put in a few years as a software engineer. Or, you might be on a completely different path and have discovered the opportunities as you witnessed the proliferation of internet use.

These days, there are generally three sectors that hire security professionals: commercial organizations, professional services, and the government, each with different entry routes.

The majority of cybersecurity experts go into a security services consulting firm. They typically come from computer science programs or have completed an advanced degree in basic security, cybercrime, or forensics. The firms might recruit from a pool of universities. You may be trained and mentored through a program at one of the Big 4 accounting firms, or a cyber-security consultancy. If you stay on the consulting route, you can become a technical lead; if you move to their business operations side, you can run the consulting team for an organization.

Other people get their start at a corporation, or a bank. As a fresh graduate, you may start on the technology side, mainly working on the network side implementing technology. From there, you could go into running and managing that technology and, later, to managing people. That's the way it normally goes for the corporates and organizations. People also transfer in and out as they do in other professions, so someone from IT auditing may go into security and another from the compliance part of the practice may go into security.

Lastly, there's working for the government, where you might start right out of graduate school and go straight into a security training program within government. Those who stay in this segment do so because they believe in the mission. From there, you might work your way up into a management position.

What to specialize in

Whether or not you already have a computer sciences background, you still need to decide on the type of security to specialize in. Do you want to focus on hacking, breaking into systems, security testing? Or forensics, systems management, which is operational, and manage security appliances? Or risk compliance, which is driving policy and strategy where technical ability doesn't need to be as deep, but you need to be able to understand all the standards and be able to write and implement policies and procedures? Because cybersecurity is a subset of computer science, specializing in different areas means having different skillsets and aptitudes. Areas of specialization include cloud security, network security, security analysis, data security etc. For more details on how to carve a path of your own, make sure to read the profiles in Chapter 7.

COMMON TITLES AND RESPONSIBILITIES

Here's a list of various cybersecurity roles and responsibilities you could start from, depending on your raw talent and/or experience:

- **Information Security Analyst**: These are the gatekeepers of an organization's information. They monitor logs, computer traffic, and periodic data to identify, report, and carry out security measures to protect an organization from breaches.

- **Security engineer**: As intermediate-level employees, they build and maintain IT security solutions. They configure firewalls and intrusion detection systems, develop security for the organization's systems and projects, and handle any technical problems that arise.

- **Security Architect**: A senior employee who builds and maintains an organization's computer, network, and infrastructure security. They have varied technical skills (SO 27001/27002, ITIL and COBIT frameworks) and a deep understanding of operating systems and risk assessment procedures and may be part of the Incident Response team.

- **Security Manager**: A mid-level manager who works with a director or CISO to execute an organization's IT policy. They also test and deploy new security tools and should have strong leadership and communication skills.

- **Security Consultant**: Experienced practitioners that are experts in the A to Z of security domains from Identity/Access Management to Software Security. They may be employed internally or externally and provide advice and solutions for their clients.

- **Penetration Tester**: Also known as ethical hackers, they hack and probe into organizations' networks, servers, applications, and software to detect and patch security flaws and vulnerabilities.

- **Incident Responder**: A cyber firefighter who assesses security threats, vulnerabilities, and incidents and is responsible for addressing them.

- **Computer Forensics Expert**: A digital detective who gathers network and infrastructure data to investigate cybercrime incidents and may work with law enforcement to gather evidence. They're adept at operating systems, forensics software, and cryptography.

- **Chief Information Security Officer (CISO)**: They're mainly responsible for overseeing the operations of an organization's IT security and staff. They're also in charge of strategies to help the organization from being breached and oversee security technology deployment. To learn more about a CISO's role and responsibilities, read the profile in Chapter 7.

Degree or no degree?

You might be wondering whether or not you need a computer science degree. The short answer is that it depends on what part of security you want to get into. Companies no doubt prefer you to have a degree. I don't have a preference either way, and I've worked with some of the best hackers in the world—many didn't have a degree. They're self-taught and can go toe-to-toe with others who have degrees.

That said, don't quit your computer science program if you're currently enrolled in one; you'll have a foundation in programing, computer engineering, information science, software development, and databases. And if your interest lies in the highly technical aspects of cybersecurity, or you want to eventually go into management and supervise teams, a computer science degree will be useful.

CERTIFICATIONS

Even if you don't always need a degree to get your foot in the door, some certifications offer advanced cybersecurity knowledge through IT industry associations. With a few years under your belt, you can take certification exams such as the Certified Information Security Manager (CISM) to specialize in IT security management; the Certified Information Systems Auditor (CISA) if you're interested in audit control and monitoring information systems; the Certified Information Systems Security Professional (CISSP) for advanced knowledge of designing, engineering, implementing and managing security for enterprises; or the Certified Cloud Systems Professional (CCSP) for advanced knowledge of cloud technology, to name a few. If you're interested in an entry-level certification, the Certified Ethical Hacker (CEH) can also be a starting point. These certifications don't necessarily include a practical element; they're designed to test a candidate's knowledge of theory.

How to start with a degree

To become any type of security professional, you'll need a broad scope of skills and technical ability, but it's possible to achieve both with a combination of formal and informal education and training.

1. If you're in high school, get exposure to science and technology education early. Some secondary schools offer a STEM-centric curriculum for students who want to see where it can take them

2. If you're contemplating college or university, take STEM courses early.

3. From there, apply to internship programs to acquire hands-on experience and hone your technical skills, and mentorship programs with STEM professionals.

4. Volunteering to run infrastructure for charities and not-for-profits can also help you get practical hands-on experience.

The non-degree path

Don't be disheartened; you can create your own path by using some of the following resources.

1. Take online courses, including certification exams.

2. Read books such as *Hacking Exposed*, the bible in the hacking community, as well as many others available on Amazon.

3. Practice building your own enclosed technical environments (closed off from the internet) to experiment and hack around. This doesn't mean you're hacking on the internet, but rather, around your own safe network. It also means that you shouldn't mess around with your next-door neighbor's Wi-Fi or your school's infrastructure equipment.

4. Don't underestimate other fields of study. A traditional background isn't always the only way in and you don't always need to uproot your life to switch careers.

   - If you have a military or police background it means you already have experience in keeping an environment safe. You would then need to add computer skills to become a good candidate to cross over to cybersecurity.

   - Psychological education can help you better understand the social psychology-motivation, behavior change, manipulation and social engineering techniques behind cyberattacks.

   - Speaking different languages is obviously useful when traveling to foreign countries.

5. Apply for internships, mentorships, and to work for non-profits.

Perks, quirks, and misconceptions

With such high demand AND a limited pool of qualified candidates, cybersecurity today almost guarantees that you can work from virtually anywhere, in any sector, and have job security. The pay in cybersecurity is also attractive. For a better idea on median annual salaries, check out sites such as Indeed.com and PayScale.com.

It's also an interesting and exciting profession. I've found that the majority of the time no two days or clients are the same. And because of the growing need for certain skills as we continue to move toward a digital economy, we also help up-skill a country's capabilities to help other nations to protect their infrastructures.

Because many companies do their best to contain details of leaks about a breach from the general public, most people don't understand what cybersecurity specialists do. I sometimes hear jokes such as, "You guys break into the system to generate business" or "You must be the ones releasing these viruses so that you can stay in business." Meanwhile, although clients think it's a pain in the ass, they know that penetration tests are necessary. Of course, if they already secured everything by design, they don't need us to test. But that rarely happens.

Then, there are the Incident Response clients who, by the time they engage us, have tried everything they can and are now in desperate need of our help. (And they are very grateful for any help we give them.) On the testing side, a vulnerability is a vulnerability, plain and simple. The worst thing that happens is that the client will need to fix something, which means they may have to delay a launch or temporarily modify part of their business while they remedy the issue. But in IT forensics or IR, getting a client to follow a structured approach that works—and relinquishing control of the situation to a point where they can trust that you're not going to screw things up— is a soft rather than technical skill. This is a typical scenario in IR.

And, if you're young, have the technical skills, and like to travel, the consulting side will likely appeal to you. If you're happy to jump on a flight and travel the world on assignments, you'll find it exciting.

Finally, if you do follow this path, you can find yourself "living in it" as I do, and because of the fast pace of living in the moment, it can be wearing. You're always working at the leading edge of technical creativity and destruction as well as seeing the best and worst of human nature. It's not an easy profession to stomach, and not for the faint hearted! Breaches are now the norm, and fixing or preventing them eventually becomes yours. There's also usually a political issue around resolving breaches. So, although we all know what should be done, we can't always solve every problem, which can also be frustrating.

Top skills and traits of successful cybersecurity specialists

I hope to have made it clear by now that a successful career in cybersecurity requires more than just a keen interest in technology. Here's my list of skills and traits of successful cybersecurity specialists, based on today's realities.

1. **It's about people as well as computers.** The ability to work in a team, and to collaborate effectively with various business units and stakeholders (e.g., HR, sales, marketing, operations) is as critical as acquiring technical skills.

2. **Be flexible and willing to travel.** Incident response work is reactive and this means last minute travel and changes to plans. I was once part of a team on our way to Indonesia, but we were stopped from boarding the plane because they were in the middle of a coup. Marshal law had been imposed and our security team advised us not to leave.

3. **Maintain tact and diplomacy.** When you travel to developing countries or across nation-states, you must be able to function professionally in any type of situation. For instance, you should know not to try to shake hands with females, even if they're married, when visiting certain Islamic countries. You should already understand their cultural norms before you land at your destination. Cultural awareness is critical; don't bring your Western ways or other cultural ways to the task, or vice versa.

4. **Confidentiality is crucial.** I once had a client who sold what I'll describe as high-end luxury services to exclusive, wealthy people. Naturally, they were worried about sharing their clientele list, which included personal information, including where they lived and their preferences. Part of the testing we performed was to see if someone could access the list. So, we received the list and yes, it was quite interesting, but only the engagement team had access to the data, and they were required to keep it confidential.

5. **The importance of communication skills.** For example, to be successful in Incident Response, you should be able to work well under pressure and relay information—good or bad—to clients, all while conducting the investigation.

6. **Keep current.** In a technical career, you need to keep up with standards and technology; for a management career, you should stay on top of the news and current public breaches.

7. **Empathy and compassion go a long way.** When responding to breaches, you need to be able to relate to the people you are working with—they are well aware they have a serious issue, and someone may lose their job.

Outlook

While I was at Mandiant, we had a hard time finding talent whom we could train and get to a skill level to work on IRs on the scale that we worked on. I searched for and hired the best and brightest IR people from Norway, Sweden, and throughout other parts of Europe, as well as the Middle East, Japan, Singapore, the Philippines, and Australia. It's possible that hiring managers across the globe were fighting to hire the very same people. Their governments may have been trying to hold on to them, but they couldn't, because they typically don't pay this level of talent well enough. If you passionately believe in helping to protect a country or organizational cyber infrastructure with a small side benefit of becoming a member of one of the highest paid and sought-after talent pool in a highly competitive field, it's a pretty sweet deal.

Endnotes
1 A copy of the technical report has been reproduced in full in the Appendix and it is also available to download from www.born2hack.life.

7

Expert Profiles

Chapter Summary

Gain insights from other successful colleagues and be inspired by their paths into cybersecurity.

By now, you know a lot about my journey and how I came into this career. Insight into other people's paths can give you a broader understanding of cybersecurity as a career. I thought I'd share the spotlight with other successful colleagues, all of whom have a unique path to this industry and whose areas of expertise vary as much as their journey.

1. **Tony Cole**, Chief Technology Officer in a company

2. **Ramses de Beer**, Incident Response in a corporation

3. **Patrick Olsen,** Security Operations in government

4. **Robert Coles**, Cybersecurity in a corporation

Tony Cole – CTO in a company

Tony Cole is Chief Technology Officer (CTO) of Attivo Networks Inc., a leader in deception for cybersecurity defense. An expert strategist in the cybersecurity industry, Tony has over thirty years of experience, ranging from consulting, risk assessment and mitigation, network security operations, and team building. He serves on the NASA Advisory Council. Tony also serves on the International Information System Security Certification Consortium $(ISC)^2$ board of directors and served in the U.S Army for over twenty years. In 2014, Tony was named Government Computer News' (GCN) "Industry IT Executive of the Year" and in 2015, inducted into the Wash 100 by Executive Mosaic as one of the most influential executives impacting government.

WHAT ARE YOUR RESPONSIBILITIES AT ATTIVO?

I'm in the cyber deception space, which means helping security professionals around the globe understand the need to put as much emphasis on the detection of cyber threats as on their prevention. I help shape the company to make sure we're providing solutions in that area, that we're taking care of customers, and that we're doing everything we can to help make the industry more secure than it is today.

It's a broad mix. As the CTO, I drive the vision and strategy for the company, internally and externally. So, I work with our product team, product engineering, sales, and product marketing teams to ensure we're focusing on the right solutions and properly positioning them to our customers and prospects.

I also help ensure that the customers we bring on board get the right support and that our products deliver the value they need to mitigate the impact of cyber breaches. Obviously, this is a large team effort with a lot of very talented folks building an awesome platform.

WHAT'S A TYPICAL DAY LIKE FOR YOU?

That's also a mix of a number of things. For instance, today I helped review a presentation for a very large financial institution with another executive. I helped him ensure they're positioned properly to meet the requirements of that prospect. On an earlier call, I worked on a partner integration with some of our product engineering team and some potential partners. Later this afternoon, I'll be meeting two more companies—a potential partner and a prospect—who are interested in our technology. It really varies across the board.

YOU STARTED YOUR CAREER JUST BEFORE THE INTERNET. WHAT WERE PEOPLE'S ATTITUDES TOWARDS CYBERSECURITY?

No one thought it was important, and no one really cared about it at that time. I remember doing briefs across government to congressional members, senior executives, and government. I was an Army soldier talking about how important cybersecurity was as we connect more and more devices; the impact it could have to government, and specifically, to the military; and why they needed to apply more resources towards it. Another issue was that no one was trained in it. I was one of the first guys doing this in the military, and there simply was no pool of candidates to pull from. It's better today; however it's still an issue.

How have things changed?

I think most of them better understand the risk. But many regions around the globe still aren't at a proper level to counter simple threats. I've talked to CEOs and board members of large multinationals who think they're not a target and, therefore, believe that their lack of cybersecurity isn't a problem. They don't give it due credence, and yet many of them are compromised today and simply don't realize it because it's not been publicized by the attacker. In fact, they don't even have the infrastructure in place, or the expertise, to recognize they've been breached.

By contrast, many of the stronger economies are well aware of the risk and the threat, so there's much more recognition and resources applied to the badly needed cybersecurity architecture, training, and processes to keep an organization or a company secure.

What's the biggest challenge today?

It depends on who you are. For those nations where cybersecurity is more recognized, it's not a major challenge because the market conditions are perfect for newcomers to the industry—there's so much need but not enough skills. But in other countries, the picture is completely different because the industry isn't given the strategic importance it deserves. So, simply put, it's problematic because it's not recognized as a major issue.

It's starting to change, but it's still a challenge for companies that aren't heavy into IT even though they have an IT infrastructure.

WHAT DREW YOU TO INFORMATION SECURITY?

I was in the Army, and I had been building secure networking systems for the intelligence community for a number of years and did not want to do a short tour in the military. Every once in a while, you get sent off to a short tour, which is a year away from your family. I wanted my kids to go to the same school and graduate from the same school and not get dragged around continuously like I was as a child.

I was talking about this to my colonel. In walked another colonel who said he needed a good non-commissioned offer (NCO) to help start up the army's computer emergency response team. That's how I got into cybersecurity. I had done cryptography for many years, and built large networks; however after moving into this space, I never looked back.

YOU STARTED IN OPERATIONS MANAGEMENT BUT HAVE ALSO BEEN ON THE CLIENT SIDE AND THE PROFESSIONAL SERVICES SIDE. HOW ARE THINGS DIFFERENT FROM ONE SIDE TO THE OTHER?

When you're in the operations seat, you do it all: configure firewalls, conduct threat analyses, and try to identify a pattern of threats across the board, just to name a few, as well as build an operations team to cover all the other facets when at that time, there weren't many guidelines to do it.

When I moved to the services side, I become more focused on ensuring that our team was trained and met the requirements for all of those operational teams we were supporting around the globe.

The government side really was that broad mix of operational hands-on knowledge. Because there wasn't much training at the time, I spent weeks going through all of these different courses they had through commercial training partners to make sure I was deep enough on not just the security side, but the operational side including a lot of deep-level courses in systems administration. I needed to know how to build the deeper level of expertise on the operational side to ensure that security pieces that were built on top of that would take seed.

WHAT WAS YOUR INVOLVEMENT IN MODIFYING THE CERTIFIED INFORMATION SYSTEMS SECURITY PROFESSIONAL (CISSP) CERTIFICATION?

I helped bring the CISSP certification to SANS[1] (the original GSEC) and helped integrate it into the GSEC course. GSEC certification was SANS's lower level certification initially, a hands-on course that helps someone demonstrate that they have the real skills to operate in that role. One of the things SANS wanted to do was make the CISSP certification a part of the one-week course work. I helped write some of the CISSP elements into that body of work.

Is there a path to become a CTO in cybersecurity team?

A number of former colleagues and friends have asked me how to become a CTO. If you're a young person going into college, it's probably a bit easier because you can pick up a major in security architecture and your journey can certainly lead you to a CTO-like role. But this also depends on what CTO role you end up taking because these roles are defined differently in different organizations. Some companies are mostly focused on the client side, where they're helping create a large architecture for the customer. In this case, you're likely to be more internally focused on the product side—defining and creating a product strategy across the company. Sometimes those CTOs own the product management functionality as well as the engineering functionality. In some companies, you may be an evangelist for the company as a CTO, working with customers and the industry as a whole. Others are mixed between the two; the CTO role varies a lot in different organizations.

There are more choices in the universities than before. I think the best thing somebody could do is go to college and focus on cybersecurity architecture. From there, they can choose which route the want and what type of CTO role they want.

Are there misconceptions about the industry?

There are many. For example, someone might think they want to enter the industry, and because of the skills gap, they'll make a lot of money. What they don't realize is that this is one of the most all-consuming fields you can go into, where your work not only gets in your blood and excites you but also doesn't stop. There's no disconnecting. There's always a new threat, and everyone wants you to engage all the time. There are probably more people on vacation who are glued to a phone or an iPad in this field than any other field I can think of. People need to be cognizant of this going into it.

WHAT ARE THE ADVANTAGES OF FOLLOWING THIS PATH?

They're significant. First, a good chunk of companies across the board want to be on the cutting edge, so you're always looking at new technology and are deeply involved in understanding the risk associated with your IT assets. Second, unlike other careers where things can get stale, this field allows you to constantly expand your knowledge. Another significant advantage is you can literally pack up and move to most major cities anywhere around the globe and get a job, even if you don't speak the language. There aren't enough cybersecurity experts, and salaries are fantastic—a young person coming out of college and an internship can probably jump right in at close to six figures if they have some operational experience. There are very few career fields where you can do that.

WHO MAKES A GREAT CTO?

From a CTO perspective, a CTO should be someone who knows that they don't know it all, that's very important. I typically learn something from everyone on our team—at all levels in most interactions. Listening is an underrated skill and it is critically important to listen to everybody on the team as a CTO, and to have a broad understanding, not only of the CISO and CIO issues, but of technology across the board so you can keep your company up to speed.

You should have a broad perspective from operational and services experiences. If you don't understand the problem set from a customer perspective, you're not going to be able effectively help customers. Understanding the different aspects of business is also very beneficial.

WHAT WOULD YOU DO DIFFERENTLY IF YOU WERE STARTING TODAY?

I more than likely would've gone into security engineering and focused on architecture as well and followed the same path. People think I'm this really smart guy who got in this early, but I was just lucky and smart enough to recognize an opportunity when it was in front of me. There's an enormous opportunity today for a young person who wants to go in this field.

ANY ADVICE TO SOMEONE ENTERING THE FIELD?

It's a phenomenal space for people to get into. But once you step in, it's all-consuming for your career. I can't state how many friends who've gone to a successful IP or acquisition, did well in the company, and then said, "I'm out, I'm out." And a year later, they're in another start-up for another company and back in the game. Cybersecurity gets in your blood, so if you want an exciting place to be, this is absolutely it.

How did you get appointed to NASA?

To my surprise, someone had recommended me to the NASA administrator. They called and appointed me to join NASA Advisory Council's Institutional Committee (NAC) to advise on cybersecurity and all its related facets related to the institutional committee's activity. This included IT and mission for NASA, and all of their stuff on the on the facilities and operational sides.

After about a year, they phased out that committee, and the NASA administrator called me, and I was moved up to the NASA Advisory Council. This has been in place for about a year, and it's been an absolute blast. The Council is led by General (Ret.) Lester Lyles, who is the chairman and a great guy. The group is a mix of PhDs, who are experts in specific areas, and a reporter, former CNN reporter Miles O'Brien, who has given great advice in that area, while I focus primarily on cybersecurity.

But what's really fun is that we're cybersecurity experts who get to learn about heliophysics and different things that these program managers brief us on, and I get to think about how to ensure that the systems can't be compromised. For me, it's been an absolute blast. We're advisors to the NASA Administrator, which to me, is extremely cool.

Do you believe countries, including the US, are equipped to protect their countries against cyberattacks?

Today, no. But given the right time and resources, I think they could build up to that structure and do it properly. Right now, the US just doesn't have that capability.

WOULD RUSSIA BEAT THE U.S. IN THE EVENT OF A CYBER WAR?

The challenge is the U.S. has done a phenomenal job, for a country this size, of taking full advantage of the digital economy, and because of that, we're highly reliant on that digital economy as a major driver of our current GDP, as it is today. So, we're much more vulnerable to cyberattacks than many other countries.

Russia at least has a digital economy, but how do you counter the North Korean threat? Everybody talks about doing cyber-attacks against North Korea, but to what end? Most attackers aren't sitting inside North Korea, they're in other countries attacking the US and other nations. They have little infrastructure and very little reliance on a global digital economy, so there's a little impact. So today, Russia would take us out, and I think some other countries could as well, if we went into a full-scale, digital cyber-war.

IN THE US, THERE'S A NEW MOVE FOR THE ARMY, NAVY, AND AIR FORCE TO JOIN THE CYBER COMMAND——IS THIS A GOOD THING?

I think it's great and was highly needed. The services won't change except to support and feed CyberCom [United States Cyber Command]. Cyber is now a domain, recognized even by NATO, so it's a critically important step forward that would help them scale up to meet threats from Russia, China, North Korea, Iran, and others. It will be very beneficial as they scale and get more resources and capability.

Speed is also an element. I think that putting cyber command as a combatant command[2] is fantastic, because all the services will feed this organization and have their own forces supporting in a dual-hat role, so there will be many more shared experiences through CyberCom, making the all of the services even smarter in this space.

I'VE PARTICIPATED IN MANY RESPONSES WHERE IT WAS CLEAR THAT THE GOVERNMENT CAN'T PROTECT ITSELF FROM BASIC THINGS LIKE GRIPTOWER. DO YOU THINK THEY'LL EVER SOLVE THIS PROBLEM?

I was in Asia years ago, and they were keen to start getting up to speed on cyber, but they were still way behind the curve. There was an attempted coup and then riots, and priorities suddenly changed. It was all about physical security at that point, so that's what they focused on. Cities and localities have the same challenges, but on a much smaller scale, and of course they're not ready because they're not normally attacked in their minds. A lot of them have a pretty long way to go, and they're under-resourced as well, so they may not know if they were breached. It's part of the challenge—it's never happened here, so should we focus on this possibility? They don't look at it as a true risk.

Part of the challenge is showing them enough studies around the globe so that they'll understand the potential risk if they don't prepare. I think that some of the efforts DHS has done in the past could potentially help some of the funding that they're doing on election security, because any awareness in one specific area for those localities and cities could help expand the knowledge base, as well as building the scale levels around the globe. There would be more security experts to come in and help. But we're a long way from there—before things gets better. But they will get better.

WHAT ARE YOUR THOUGHTS ON A CITIZEN'S RIGHT TO PRIVACY, INCLUDING THEIR OWN SOCIAL MEDIA?

As hard as this is to say, Cambridge Analytica did a service to the American public. Before this issue hit the news, the vast majority of citizens would all complain about government snooping on them. At the same time, this is the same public that has freely given away ten times more data to Facebook, Google, Twitter, Instagram, and Snapchat without any concern for their privacy.

I'm hopeful that out of this event comes a better awakening in the public and that they'll understand that it's not just the government that we should continue to try to monitor, but also massive tech corporations that collect all of our data continuously. Today, we willingly giving them data in exchange for free services. I'm hopeful that this will change the business models of some of these large tech companies as well. Can they continue to drive revenue without selling or sharing everybody's data or storing everything across the board, while ensuring that customers understand when they're sharing something?

Apple recently updated their iOS. It's going to be a big pop-up warning with two people shaking hands, and when you try to install a new app or update one, it will ask, "This app is asking for the following information... Are you really sure you want do this?" It's prominent enough that people may actually read it and think about it before they just say "Sure, go ahead."

Do you believe security has improved from ten or fifteen years ago to now?

Generally speaking, yes. There are more gaps, and putting together a good security architecture is more complex. And some business verticals are finally taking the risk seriously. But we now have more capability than ever.

We all know that there's a determined adversary that wants to break into our systems and will raise their level of sophistication as needed to get over whatever hurdles you put in their way. We still don't have enough on the detection side to quickly detect those breaches when they do take place. But I think we've done a tremendous job overall of increasing the cybersecurity awareness for a number of industries and governments around the globe. As the saying goes, "It's a marathon, not a sprint."

What would you change about this industry?

Everyone needs to understand that they are at risk and that they need to do the proper things based on their role within their organization. I wouldn't focus on my organization or cybersecurity in general to make things better. I would do what I've been doing and try to get more people involved—training kids as young as kindergarten and teachers about the do's and don'ts of cybersecurity. Then, get every high school and university that works in technology to start teaching secure coding at the lowest levels, as an integral part of the course. These things could have a significant impact on what we look like in fifteen to twenty years.

WHAT COMES AFTER YOU'VE BEEN CTO?

I'm having great fun where I am today and don't plan any changes. Someday I might jump to another exciting start-up if I find one. Who knows, perhaps I'll be semi-retired and may do a little consulting, or a little board work. I'll also spend more time with my wonderful grandkids and family.

Endnote
1. SANS Institute is the most trusted resource for information security training, cybersecurity certifications, and research.
2. Combatant command are forces from at least two US military departments.

Ramses de Beer — Incident Response in a corporation

Ramses de Beer started tinkering with electronics when he was about eight years old. His parents bought a computer a couple of years later and he began experimenting with it just before the general public started getting online. Those early days led him to study computer science and carve a career in IT.

Today, he's Senior Security Engineer and Incident Response (IR) Manager at Google EMEA, based in Zurich. He's a forensic expert with a breadth of experience that includes consultancy, incident response management, and network defense/offense operations. A well-traveled expert, Ramses speaks Dutch, English, French, German, and Spanish.

WHAT ARE YOUR MAIN RESPONSIBILITIES?

I investigate potential security issues at Google and Google Services. I also manage teams during those investigations and head certain tool development projects.

WHAT INITIALLY DREW YOU TO INFORMATION SECURITY?

My first job came when I answered a newspaper ad. Back then, the term hacker didn't necessarily mean someone breaking into things; it was a generic term for people who like to tinker with hardware and software. The justice department in the Netherlands wanted to recruit hackers to investigate legal cases, so I answered the ad, got the job, and have never looked back.

I stayed at the Netherlands Forensic Institute for about two years and then moved to the Ministry of the Interior. There I spent twelve and a half years performing computer network operations mainly on the offensive side. From there, I went into the oil industry (at Shell) and did consultancy at Mandiant before moving in-house at Google. It's been a ride—consultancy, government, consultancy, and then in-house commercial space, corporate.

What's a typical day like for you at Google?

I get up quite early to do my morning routine and get in the office around 9:30 to 10 a.m.. The office is typically dead before 10 a.m., as most people get in around that time. There are usually meetings because we have offices across multiple time zones and staff in Sydney, Zurich, and Sunnyvale. We then have operational meetings, and then there are two possibilities—either I do project work, which means we're programming, designing, or working with the engineering team to build incident response tools, or we have on-call schedules.

We're essentially a line of defense for Google, so if there are potential security or privacy issues, our team is paged. We have on-call rotation schedules that I also participate in, which means any one of us can be paged by anyone within Google anywhere in the world when there's an issue. Because we're not the first line of defense, the issues we face have already been escalated and need IR experts, and they can be technical in nature and involve a PR/Communications response, a legal response, or involvement from other parties.

WHAT IS THE LIFE CYCLE OF AN IR INVESTIGATION?

A typical response is either privacy-or security-related. First, we need to dig in and know which type it is. Google is a huge company with many different products and services, and you need to get the right people together to understand the problem. We usually plan conference calls to figure out what's going on. At that moment, I take the lead and start managing that crisis, which means delegating tasks and control progress across those tasks.

If I'm leading an investigation, I always involve another team member to execute the investigative work. An investigation can take day a day, a few weeks, or months. We also figure out if and when to involve the legal, communications, and marketing teams to know how to address our customers. Then, we wrap up with a post-mortem where we track those activities across Google and make sure the required improvements are implemented.

YOU'VE MOVED AROUND FROM CLIENT SIDE AS AN IT CONSULTANT TO SERVICES AT MANDIANT, AND THEN INTO IT ON THE CLIENT SITE. HOW DID YOU EVENTUALLY CHOOSE THE IR SIDE AFTER SPENDING SO MANY YEARS IN GOVERNMENT?

After twelve and a half years in the government and moving from unit to unit about every three years, I thought it would be interesting to go into Incident Response. I'd remained sane (which can be a challenge when working in government), kept learning, and after being mostly on the offensive side, I wanted to use my knowledge in the defensive side and help defend organizations. I wanted to explore different environments, different customers, and see how I could grow. Mandiant came at the right time because they were among the top companies doing IR at that time.

YOU'VE WORKED IN A NUMBER OF LOCATIONS—ENGLAND, THE NETHERLANDS, DUBAI, SWITZERLAND, AND IN ASIA. WHAT'S YOUR FAVORITE PLACE TO WORK AND WHY?

Wherever my wife and children happen to be is always my favorite place. From a professional perspective, I really enjoyed the Middle East. It's culturally challenging, and you get to address actors from the Five Eyes[1] (FVEY) group which is also challenging and interesting. I'm also partial to warm weather and enjoy the multicultural aspect of the Middle East, which has made me grow tremendously.

Google is flexible in how you perform your work, and I think it works if you can handle yourself and are results-driven. I like to see the team and see them face-to-face, so I try to be in the office as much as possible. I do sometimes take time to work from the Netherlands because that's where my family lives.

IS THERE A TYPICAL PATH FOR SOMEONE WHO WANTS TO GO INTO INCIDENT RESPONSE?

There was no educational path before, but now there is. The educational path geared toward forensics is computer science or security engineering. Then you can start into forensics— computer or digital forensics— and get involved in investigations.

Once you've acquired some experience, it's easy to move into Incident Response. I don't think you can start in Incident Response or incident management because you need some experience first.

What makes a great IR specialist?

The greatest IR specialists I've learned from are those who have perfect balance between their technical skills and their people skills. They've learned to be the (stereotypical) person under the hoodie working on his own, but also the person in a room full of people to whom they can communicate on every level, be it the technical person sitting next to them or the C-level executive sitting across the table.

An IR specialist needs to understand forensics on different levels (i.e., system level, network, PR) as well as what different stakeholders need to hear to be able to condense and translate technical skills and technical investigations. Because you're leading the investigation and not doing or solving everything yourself, you need to understand who you need and when.

What advice would you give to someone entering the field now?

You should be adaptable and ready to be in the type of environment where a peak or crisis can happen at any time. If you're the type of person who likes peaking and then downtime instead of a constant workload, you should go for it. You should also have a technical background, but you don't have to be a forensic guru to start. Lastly, you need people skills—or a social sciences background—to handle the stressful situations, read people, and understand how they behave.

ARE THERE ANY MISCONCEPTIONS ABOUT WHAT CYBERSECURITY EXPERTS DO?

Many young people are scared off because they have this idea that you should be a huge nerd, tinkering with computer from a very young age to actually do this, which is not true. You can do this from 9 to 5, not take on any side projects, and not work on this stuff 24/7, and still be successful.

Another misconception is that you need to become a manager or have a leadership role to grow. But leading is something you do at every level—as a nerd or as a social person in a crisis—so you don't need a title, but rather, take responsibility and find opportunities to lead at every level.

WHAT ARE SOME OF THE ADVANTAGES OR BENEFITS OF FOLLOWING THIS PATH?

In this world, the learning never stops. So, if you're eager to learn and use your creativity, this is definitely the field to get in to. You'll learn from technical challenges, from the different types of customers, and corporate and country cultures. And the work never stops, so there are a huge opportunities for anybody who wants to grab it and go for it.

WOULD YOU DO ANYTHING DIFFERENTLY IF YOU WANTED TO FOLLOW THIS PATH TODAY?

I probably wouldn't have had a formal education. I went to school in the Netherlands, which I think was extremely overrated.

Although I studied computer science, I don't think I learned that much—most of my learning was autodidactic, so if I had to do it again, I would probably skip the formal education. (That's not necessarily the advice I'd give others, though.)

WHAT ABOUT CERTIFICATIONS?

They measure not only a certain base level of knowledge, but it tells me that this person is focused enough and has the backbone to do what's needed to finish the certification. And in this business, there's a boatload of certifications from very generic overviews of varying (information) security topics, to different technical courses, and at different levels. But certifications are just a starting point, and it's up to the interviewers to test your day-to-day problem-solving skills, and most certifications will not help you there. You still need the experience.

WHAT ARE THE PROS AND CONS OF WORKING IN THE GOVERNMENT, A CONSULTANCY, OR A TECH COMPANY?

Let's start with the government. To me, the government is both interesting and annoying. It's interesting because you have an immense amount of time, freedom to develop your skills, and it's not results-driven culture. So, these are a positive if you start your career and want to develop your skills—there's no pressure and you have an immense amount of time, and usually funding, to pay for your skills development. The most negative aspect is that it's slow. Because it's slow, you won't get promoted or further your career easily, which can get very frustrating. You need to know what you're getting into. I tell people to make sure they move internally every two and a half to three years to stay sane.

Consultancy is great if you want to work in a high stress environment, meet new people, and deal with new technical challenges and environments each week. It's a very fast learning and grooming school where you can also improve your people skills.

As to the negative aspects, you should have more maturity and be able to handle yourself in this high-stress environment. There's usually a great deal of travel and demanding customers, which can cause burnout, so you need to know when to slow down. I tell people who want to start out in consultancy that they'll gain a ton of experience, but it will be compressed in a week instead of five years.

The positive side of working for corporate organizations is that they have standard procedures and policies in place. So, you land into a framework where they think for the long-run and you can focus on your job and instead of procedural policy creation. The con is that all these procedures can hamper your creativity. If you want to work at a bigger corporation, make sure you get your hands dirty. Pick up some projects that will allow you to express your creativity and keep your skills sharp. Otherwise, you may get sucked up into the bigger multinational policy worlds and end up in the same job until you retire (which is okay if you want that!).

Consumers are becoming more and more aware of the privacy challenges when using internet services on a daily basis.

On the commercial side, companies are improving constantly in the privacy and security space to balance three things. First, they need to make profit. Second, they need to keep users happy. Lastly, companies are working to improve their products to address the privacy challenges, but they still need to make money, so balancing their big data repository with the growing awareness of privacy issues will be a continual challenge.

I think the next three to five years will usher in some very big changes and consumers will become more aware of the balance between using the internet and privacy and sharing information.

WHAT HASN'T CHANGED?

Basic internet is still strung together with ancient technologies. For example, we have DNS—a backbone technology and the phonebook of internet—that, in its simplest form, translates Web addresses like www.example.com to an IP address. That's a very ancient technology that has hardly changed in twenty to twenty-five years. Some basic components of the internet that we now rely on to perform financial transactions or store medical data are still the same. We'll need to change a few of those basic building blocks to get to an internet where governments, corporations, and customers feel confident about sharing things. Companies and researchers need to address the basic building block issues to get on a higher level and keep the growth sustainable.

ARE THERE AREAS WHERE WE'RE IMPROVING?

As an industry, we've brought the security knowledge and focus up to board level. That's a big gain. The focus of external organizations on privacy and security issues is also deeper, and I think that's where our industry has grown in the last twenty years.

But we're still a long way from where we need to be. We need to understand that the privacy and security industry needs to take own its responsibility; the board level needs to enable them to fully ake on that role and implement good measures, so that the services we're offering are actually acceptable. We still need to fill this gap.

WHAT WOULD YOU CHANGE ABOUT THIS INDUSTRY?

Right now, different sectors of the tech industry are dictated, dominated by some very big players, and have become so big that they are more powerful than certain countries. I do not think that's the correct way forward because these companies are profit-driven. It might be good idea to split up these big monopolies. Splitting them into smaller parts would make it easier for consumers to address those companies and to actually have influence in those companies to change it in a way that's best for them. Humans want to have control themselves, but big companies usually think they know what's best for consumers. I don't know how I would split them up, nor when or who should control what, but I do see the current problem with big companies controlling large amounts of privacy-related information, having huge control over negotiations on even a national level. Since they're also steered by profits and shareholders, it's not the way to go.

WHAT IS THE GOVERNMENT'S ROLE IN PROTECTING ITS CITIZENS AND ENTERPRISES?

Government should have a significant influence. The security and privacy industry and space has grown from a niche nerd's markets to something that dictates the basic stuff in our life—financial, medical, and communications with your loved ones and when you're in crisis. I think those building blocks are so basic and important in a society that it should be the role of a civilized government to take responsibility to ensure those basic building blocks are at a certain level. But governments are slow and often playing catch-up with legislation. And multinational companies have enormous power to influence governments in different ways.

HOW DO YOU SEE THE INDUSTRY EVOLVING IN THE NEXT FIVE YEARS?

I think it will be focused on two things. First, it will become a normalized, mass consumer good that everyone can use. Second, it will be partly driven by smart algorithms, be it machine learning and artificial intelligence.

In five years, it will be driven by [new] companies that commoditize the security industry, take the specialist, "expert sauce" out of it, and combine it with a set of machine learning and artificial intelligence that will simplifies its functionalities for the users.

WHAT COMES AFTER IR? WHAT'S YOUR NEXT CAREER GOAL?

I'm a quite simple guy. I'm going keep doing my daily activities that I like doing. Sometimes, that's going to the beach having a beer with my family or friends. Other times, it's hacking away all night. Or taking the lead on a certain project or leading a team into a major incident. So, I don't know what the next step in my career will be, but I know for sure that as with all other steps so far, it will be interesting. I'll meet new people and visit interesting places and learn about more cultures, which will help me learn new things every day.

TELLS US ABOUT AN EMBARRASSING INCIDENT OR PERSONAL MESS-UP.

I've made a ton of mistakes, but here's one of the most embarrassing. Way back, when I first started, I got a call from a colleague a bit older than me.

"Ramses, tomorrow we have a discussion with our director of our department. I feel a bit sick. I can't join this conversation. Could you go instead of me? Another colleague is joining as well."

"Sure, no problem."

I never asked what it was about. So the next morning, I show up at 9 a.m., the director of the Dutch forensic institute—the top executive—is in the room, and my colleague and I sit across from him.

"I really don't know what it's about," I whispered to my colleague.

He looked at the director and said, "Well, (name of director), Ramses and I are here to tell you that we've lost trust in you, and we wanted to say that we don't want to work for you anymore as a department."

What? I had joined that organization only about six months before.

The director, who had known my colleague and had history with him, looked at me instead and asked, "Ramses, what is this about? What are you saying?"

I learned early on to always get the context of a conversation, understand who I'll be talking to, what their objective is, and not assume anything in advance. This mindset works well and helps me stay focused on what is important.

Endnote
1. FVEY is an intelligence sharing alliance comprising Australia, Canada, New Zealand, the United Kingdom and the United States.

Patrick Olsen—Security Operations in Government

Patrick Olsen was a Security Operations Center (SOC) Manager at a US Federal agency, where he was responsible for technical direction of the operations team. This interview details his experiences there.

WHAT WERE YOU RESPONSIBLE FOR AT THE US FEDERAL AGENCY?

I managed the SOC and led twenty-seven government civilians and defense contractors. We owned enterprise alerting and detection, threat hunting, incident response, digital forensics, and the malware analysis component.

Our team also provided analysis and log data, mostly from the enterprise applications and network to support Office of Personnel Responsibility (OPR), which has law enforcement [arrest] authority within the Federal agency. We did this in support of internal investigations—for example, time card fraud.

My primary responsibilities as the SOC manager was the technical direction of the overall team, which required a significant amount of mentorship. When I first started, the team wasn't well built; it was only a year old. Prior to this, someone in a leadership role decided it was a good idea to eliminate the SOC and "assume the risk," so by the time I arrived, we had to re-establish communication with cross-functional teams, start from scratch, and create myriad of SOPs and workflows. We also had to get rid of antiquated processes and start from scratch and get better visibility into the network by improving our logging capabilities and removing antiquated technology. I had a few rock star employees that made my life a lot easier, so I am forever grateful for them.

SOUNDS LIKE A COMBINATION OF TECHNICAL AND OPERATIONAL RESPONSIBILITIES. DO YOU HAVE A PREFERENCE?

At this point in my career, I prefer the operational side. I enjoy looking at a process, whether that's a technology or human workflow and finding areas that can be improved. I then like to brainstorm and come up with new ideas on how we might be able to improve it. I enjoy creating new solutions from something that doesn't exist and seeing the positive effects of that change. I like to think, "You can build the robots to replace you, or you can simply wait around until the robots replace you." At the end of the day at least I can say I improved something if I was the one that helped build the robots.

YOU STUDIED SECURITY MANAGEMENT. HOW DID YOU BECOME INTERESTED IN CYBERSECURITY?

I grew up in Columbus, Nebraska. It's a small [~20,000] blue-collar town, so we didn't have modern computer labs while I was attending high school in 1998-2001. We had core trades—welding, metals, autos, drafting, etc. For me, it just so happened that our auto mechanics teacher was a very smart guy, and as an additional duty, he was also responsible for running the school's network; which included managing Windows Active Directory (a directory based information storage), managing the file servers, etc.

I don't recall exactly how I found out he did all this extra work, but I did. I signed up for his Autos class. I signed up for his class, not because I cared about cars, but because I wanted to ask him questions about computers. So, I would show up before class, and I would stick around after class, and he would show me around Active Directory. I skipped many study halls to talk to him. I should have received an F in that class, but I got a C because I think he enjoyed talking computers with me.

My parents also made sure we had a computer at home, but I mostly used it to play games.

I don't recall how I got introduced to security, but I started to read the *Hacking Exposed* books in high school. I started an Associate's degree in Computer Networking at a Community College in Omaha, Nebraska. I obviously learned about networking, but I also started to learn more about Linux, lower levels of TCP/IP, and a sprinkle of Information Security.

Two of my four roommates were Computer Engineering students, and my brother, who also lived with us, studied Management Information Systems. We had a house of nerds. Our partment was full of computers, and as everyone became more knowledgeable about computers. I eventually started digging deeper into security.

After I completed my Associate degree, I enrolled in a Security Management bachelor's degree program at Bellevue University. This was post-9/11, and there was a lot of emphasis on security, so

I thought it was a natural progression. This program was less about IT security and more about infrastructure security, the history of security, etc. I would typically spin my homework assignments into something related to IT security, however.

After graduating, I got a job at United States Strategic Command in Bellevue, Nebraska. I didn't have a security clearance, and as a result, I was assigned the role of Configuration Management Analyst. Looking back, I think this was helpful, but I knew I wanted to be involved more in the information security space, so I moved into an Information Assurance role after receiving my Top Secret security clearance and moving to Washington D.C. at an organization called PM Night Vision/Reconnaissance, Surveillance, and Target Acquisition located on Ft. Belvoir. This was at the height of the Iraq and Afghanistan wars and we were a quick-reaction capabilities organization. We built sensor and target acquisition systems used to track the enemy along main supply routes to counter high improvised explosive device (IED) threats. Our claim to fame during that time was the fielding of a system called Base Expeditionary Targeting and Surveillance System-Combined (BETSS-C). I was responsible for ensuring the system met the required Information Assurance security requirements prior to going operational in the war zones.

In 2008, I vacationed in Japan and really enjoyed it. Coming from a small town of twenty-thousand people, I found it was neat being in a foreign country. I came home from Japan and I immediately applied for jobs in Asia. I accepted a job in Seoul, South Korea, and two weeks later I moved to Seoul. This is where I ended up doing more in "hands-on" cybersecurity work. I also started attending SANS training during this time. While living in Seoul I worked for US Eighth Army and US Special Operations Command–Korea (SOCKOR). At SOCKOR I worked on deploying Splunk, Sourcefire IDS/IPS systems, Cisco firewalls, McAfee ePO, and configuring all the rulesets for the endpoints.

Eventually, I ended up leaving the government. I took a job in Singapore with FireEye, where I was a Senior Consultant working on digital forensic and incident response investigations all over the world. After leaving FireEye, I moved back to the US and did a short stint in the technology sector at one of the world's most valuable brands.

WHAT'S THE DIFFERENCE BETWEEN A CORPORATE AND A GOVERNMENT ENVIRONMENT?

Let me first start by saying I mean no disrespect. The government, because of the unions and lack of accountability tends to be an environment that promotes meritocracy. Again, there are some really great people working for the government, so I don't want to over generalize, but from my experience with the non-bargaining units and union workers; as a manager, it is very hard and time consuming to hold underperformers accountable. It's the reason I left government. On the corporate side there is usually a financial motive so if businesses or people don't perform; the business goes out of business and likewise, the underperformers can be removed easier.

Do GOVERNMENT EMPLOYEES TEND TO BE THERE BECAUSE THEY BELIEVE IN THE MISSION, IN PROTECTING THE COUNTRY. WHAT ABOUT THE MONEY?

I think that some people truly believe in the mission and I think that's great. We need people like that. The people working at the NSA and some of our more sophisticated government agencies aren't doing it because of the paycheck. Sure, some of the defense contractors supporting them make good money, but they could make a lot more in Silicon Valley. I personally didn't choose to work in the government because I had a sense of "mission." I think some people, for example, at the NSA, do it more because what they can do there they can't do anywhere else. There are only so many places that you can effectively reach out and touch a human being via cyberspace, and that would be in some of those three letter agencies. I have to think that has some kind of draw over money. And of course, there are the brave men and women in our armed forces. Many make a choice to serve for twenty-plus years. While they get paid well and have great retirement benefits, I have to assume it's partly because of the "mission."

WHAT MAKES A GREAT SECURITY OPERATIONS MANAGER?

I'm still fairly new to this so it's hard to say. In my experience, I would say it's good to have a wide range of experience. What I mean by that is when you're leading people, someone who can only translate 1's and 0's may not be that effective at managing resources. Likewise, the inverse is true. If your only knowledge of security is a CISSP book, then your peers, especially the good ones, may not respect you.

Once you get into a role, there are other things you must do right. You must look at resources (both money and people), cross-functional relationships, team dynamics, and the realization that you can't have all the latest and greatest technology today. It can take years before funding cycles allow you the ability to implement what you want. So, you need a nice balance between understanding technical side and equally or better understanding of the soft-skills.

YOU STARTED IN IR AND THEN MOVED AROUND BETWEEN GOVERNMENT IN AN OPERATIONS ROLE TO IR ON THE SERVICES SIDE. WHY DID YOU LEAVE THE CORPORATE SECTOR AND REJOIN THE GOVERNMENT?

I started out on the consulting side in Singapore when I accepted a job at FireEye. This was my first corporate job, and it was a start-up which was exciting. When I was in Singapore, we were one hundred percent in startup mode. The company IPOd and things were moving a hundred miles an hour, and it was a lot of fun. When I moved back to the FireEye US office, that start-up "culture" seemed to die down. It was a hard adjustment. It felt like the wind left my sails, and I just started to lose interest.

I learned a lot as a consultant, but I rarely got to see the fruits of my labor. For example, we might go into an organization and contain an attacker or eradicate some malware, so operations could resume, but nothing actually got fixed.

We operate very much like an emergency room. Doctors and nurses stop the bleeding, patch things up, and transfer the patient to the intensive care unit. Sure, without the emergency room the patient dies, but the ICU staff ensures the longevity of the patient by making sure they get the root of the problem healed before the patient leaves.

I wanted to be the ICU. I wanted to use my knowledge to help organizations really make a difference and improve their security posture.

So, when I was offered a job to help build the SOC at the Federal agency, I thought it would be good experience to actually try and build something from the ground up, and take ownership of the security program.

YOU STARTED YOUR CYBERSECURITY CAREER WHEN IT HAD ALREADY BECOME A RECOGNIZED FIELD. IS THERE A CLEAR PATH TO GET INTO THE INDUSTRY?

Yes. Universities now offer Digital Forensics programs as well as minors in Cybersecurity, Information Assurance, etc. This wasn't the case when I was in college back in 2001-2006. Today, information security programs are full-fledged bachelor's or master's degree programs. If you look closely at the curricula malware analysis and incident response courses are included. You also have a lot of blogs being written about the field and good training programs like SANS offer people the training and knowledge to get their foot in the door even without a degree.

Is it the government's role to provide security for its citizens, or is it the company's role?

It depends. I don't advocate for full government takeover of security monitoring of companies. I mean, I worked at the government; there are plenty of problems there. Their networks aren't the most secure, so it's a glass house kind of discussion.

Having said that, it's probably a government responsibility to assist organizations or owners of critical infrastructure to respond to security incidents when they need it. And just like the military protecting the country and its interests in the physical world—and cybersecurity being a world in itself—someone needs to protect this virtual world. We should have some level of government intervention involvement in the cyberworld. I think this could be in mandating organizations to invest in security.

Companies have proven, from a regulation standpoint, that unless they're told to do something, they won't do it. Companies are in the business of making money so if a program isn't making them money they are not likely to do it unless they have to. They have failed time and time again. The only way you get a lot of participation from organizations is when governments mandate it. I'm not a "big brother" kind of person, but the reality is, if you don't want someone watching you, don't wait for something bad to happen. The banks failed in 2008 because no one was watching them. They shouldn't complain when the government steps in and starts imposing new regulations to make sure it doesn't happen again. Likewise, there are new multi-million record data breaches a few times a year now. Sooner or later the government will step in and start mandating security.

DO YOU THINK GOVERNMENTS ARE PROTECTING THEIR COUNTRIES' CYBERSPACE AT THE MOMENT?

I don't think so. I don't have any statistics to prove it though. I respond to way too many compromises as a consultant to think otherwise. How can they protect us if they're not hiring the right people? The US is good at attacking people but we're not good at defense.

I also don't think governments should be solely responsible for protecting their countries. It's also the company's responsibility to protect the people. If consumers are trusting these businesses with their information, which the companies are using to make a profit, I think they have a responsibility to protect the data they maintain. It's good customer service. It shouldn't take the government to make companies do this.

DO YOU THINK COMPANIES HAVE CHANGED THEIR SECURITY POSTURE SINCE YOU ENTERED THIS FIELD?

If you're asking me if I think companies have gotten better at thwarting attacks, no. I do not think they have. Sure, attackers may have to chain multiple exploits together and use more complex techniques to ultimately exploit vulnerabilities in some products, but overall, if an attacker wants in, they will get in. For example, Windows 10 offers a lot more security than Windows XP, but it's still possible to compromise Windows 10 machines. So, we have improved and raised the bar for attackers, but the attackers have adjusted as necessary.

Organizations may have slightly better visibility into their environments now, but attackers are still exploiting the same things they did ten years ago. They are exploiting poorly configured external facing servers, misconfigured external facing ports (RDP), poor password management, poor configuration management practices, the lack of two-factor authentication on external facing services, failure to patch systems in a timely manner, and most of all, they are exploiting humans via phishing emails.

WHAT ADVICE WOULD YOU GIVE TO SOMEONE ENTERING THE INCIDENT RESPONSE AND DIGITAL FORENSIC FIELD TODAY?

I would recommend two paths, but I would say that pursuing them at the same time is better. First, start learning how to code. Second, if you want to be a good incident responder, start out as a systems administrator. You need to know how systems work and how they interact together. Having a good understanding of systems administration is very helpful when responding to incidents.

I have never met a good digital forensic or incident response consultant (or analyst) that couldn't code. With the number of systems and the sizes and types of environments today, coding is necessary if you want to be good. It's even more necessary as we move into the cloud and everything is an API call.

WHAT WOULD YOU DO DIFFERENTLY YOU DECIDED TO GO INTO THIS FIELD TODAY?

I would have worked a few years as a systems administrator and I would've gone to school for software development. Then maybe I would have minored in security or just learned security as a hobby. I also would have also studied math more. As things progress towards machine learning and AI being good at math would be beneficial.

WHAT ARE THE BENEFITS OR THE ADVANTAGES OF FOLLOWING THIS PATH?

There's virtually a negative unemployment rate. Our skills aren't easily outsourced to other countries because of the criticality of the data we have access to at some of these organizations. There is also a skills shortage globally, so that prevents additional outsourcing.

The money is also good. There are not a lot of jobs where someone who is 25 years old can make six-figures after a few years of work experience.

For me personally, in addition to the money and steady employment, I was able to travel the world. I traveled all over Asia and Australia. I stood next to the pyramids in Egypt and met awesome people in Myanmar. I met my wife in South Korea. There are not a lot of jobs outside of the financial services sector that provide that lifestyle.

ANY MISCONCEPTIONS ABOUT THE CYBERSECURITY FIELD?

If you want to be good, it requires that you to spend a lot of time learning, which can get overwhelming. There's also a lot of pressure to keep up with the latest technology—a new operating system seems to be released every year. Now we have the cloud, but it's not one cloud, it's Google Cloud, Amazon Cloud, Azure Cloud. Then you have the smaller vendors and each one has a different way of doing things. Soon you will have cars and IoT devices to learn about.

I don't think people realize the level of effort that goes into being good. You need to consistently level up. If you want to be mediocre, I guess that's fine too.

WHAT IS NEXT FOR YOU?

I'm a laid-back person, so I tend to roll with the punches. I find that when I plan for things they never pan out, so I stopped. I moved to Asia for a year and ended up staying for six while living in two different countries so I have learned not to plan too far ahead and just see how things go.

Robert Coles—Cybersecurity in a corporation

Robert Coles was the Chief Information Security Officer (CISO) for GlaxoSmithKline (GSK), which is the fifth largest global pharmaceutical, consumer healthcare and vaccines company in the world, operating in about 120 countries. Robert's experience includes CISO at National Grid (US/UK electricity and gas company), CISO at Merrill Lynch, various information security leadership roles at Royal Bank of Scotland, and Partner in Charge of Information Security at KPMG. After earning PhD in psychology, he continues his research as a visiting professor at Royal Holloway, University of London.

WHAT WERE YOUR RESPONSIBILITIES AT GSK?

I was accountable for GSK's cybersecurity and information security risk. I oversaw several teams—the Security Operations team (SOC application security, patching, access management); the technical security consultants (subject matter experts) who handled systems development, setting requirements, and checking them when the applications were procured or developed; third-party oversight experts who handled contract negotiations when we bought services that managed our sensitive information; incident responders (24/7 forensics, investigations, etc.,); security strategy and architecture; and governance, risk management, and office of the CISO responsibilities. Lastly, I oversaw a change program, which is a team of 80–120 capital and OPEX people who deliver change and strategy within the organization.

You studied finance and psychology; how did you get started in information security?

I went to university for a short period, and then I dropped out and became an accountant. I joined KPMG in the late 80s as part of the computer audit team but ended up doing programming for the first two years to analyze financial data from large bank mainframe-based systems.

During this time, I also stumbled across Unix, and I started to help the development of a building society mortgage and investment system. I learnt how to get to the Unix command line to extract the data from the system to be able to analyze it. I learned more about its different flavors, varieties, and vulnerabilities–and how to secure them. Unix was nascent at that time and difficult to secure. I started to sell that knowledge as a consultant, first within Leeds, then across the north of England. Then, I started to learn security in other operating systems, which is something KPMG realized they could also sell. They eventually developed a team across northern England; meanwhile I moved down to London and got a partnership with them.

Around that time, I became interested in psychology, mainly because of the vast amount of work I was undertaking in the health and finance sectors, and I noticed that there were marked differences in the attitude towards security across these sectors. In the health sector, if you get the data wrong, you can kill someone, while in the financial sector, you know it's only money! There should have been more focus in the health sector, but it was the complete opposite. It got me thinking about why people think so differently in different sectors, so years later, I ended up doing a PhD on the psychology of risk and security, developing a psychometric tool to elucidate mental models and comparing individuals within the two sectors over two time periods.

WHAT WAS A TYPICAL DAY LIKE FOR YOU?

There were no typical days; almost every day was different. When I joined the organization, my job was to work out how much security was enough and create and cost strategy. That took me about six months. I then got some funding, and my next task was to build the change team and the business-as-usual team.

Once those teams were in place, it was about delivering the strategy and the business-as-usual activity of managing incidents, making sure that we had the right contract terms with third parties and the right level of security in the software.

Then, it was on to building a governance infrastructure to give me oversight of all the security activities because I was the first CISO in the organization. Lastly, I managed operations. So, the days weren't standard, but varied, which is one of the things I loved about that job.

WHAT DID YOU MOST ENJOY ABOUT THIS ROLE?

I fundamentally enjoy learning how a complex large organization works, developing a strategy, building a team, and delivering the strategy. Once the strategy and direct reports are in place, things become very operational, and that's a different kind of job.

WHAT ASPECTS DID YOU ENJOY LEAST?

Organizational bureaucracy and having to wait to make changes. Large organizations don't like change, as it brings risk and effort, and that can make work difficult for some people.

ARE THERE MISCONCEPTIONS ABOUT WHAT CYBERSECURITY SPECIALISTS DO?

I don't think the general public has a good understanding of it, nor of their personal risk; if they did, they wouldn't keep on clicking on phishing links, which is why some criminals are so successful.

WHAT DO YOU LOOK FOR IN A NEW HIRE?

Decent security qualification, such as a master's or an Institute of Information Security Professionals (MInstISP) certification, which tells me that this person is taking their career and security seriously enough to want to invest in education for themselves. I also look at the previous positions they've held and evidence that they've done the type of things I need doing.

WHICH SPECIFIC TRAITS DO YOU LOOK FOR?

Someone who wants to do strategy should be a visionary and able to see the big picture. Someone entering governance and compliance should be enquiring, process orientated, detailed and meticulous. For systems development, a candidate should be knowledgeable and want to keep up with new technologies and threats. For all roles, good negotiating skills are paramount.

WHAT ADVICE WOULD YOU GIVE SOMEONE WHO WANTED TO EVENTUALLY BECOME A CISO?

There's no rule about where to start. If you want to be a CISO, you ideally want to have worked within all of the functions in security. This way, you'll get to know what all of those functions do. I would say it's much easier to manage a function when you've worked in it yourself. Make sure that you get a breadth of experience, as well as depth.

WHAT ABOUT ADVANCED CERTIFICATES SUCH AS THE CEH (CERTIFIED ETHICAL HACKER) OR THE CISM (CERTIFIED INFORMATION SECURITY MANAGER)?

Information security certifications are OK, but mostly they just prove you have a good memory. They don't usually test competence or prove that you can actually do the job! Some exams like CEH or CISM required proof from an employer that you have done the job for a number of years. I helped set up the CISM exam at the Information Systems Audit and Control Association (ISACA). In one of the first exams, a young man took the test and passed it. We all thought we had made it too easy, but it turns out that he was just very bright and had a great memory. But he still couldn't qualify as a CISM because he needed work experience, which he got a few years later.

Other certificates, like the Institute of Information Security Professionals "member" status require a viva with an experienced interviewer who probes for both knowledge and competence, and this gives a much better indication of skill.

DID YOU EVER THINK THAT YOU WOULD END UP AS CISO OF A LARGE COMPANY?

I've never planned my career. But what I have done is spot opportunities and had the courage to take a few risks for what look like interesting and exciting jobs. The circumstances have worked out and gotten me to where I am.

DO YOU FIND THAT BOARDROOMS DON'T UNDERSTAND TECHNOLOGY OR SECURITY?

I've had great engagement with CEOs, the executive, and the PLC (public limited company) board, and some of these individuals are former members of other boards or heads of other companies. The meetings tend to be challenging with difficult questions from very knowledgeable people. Achieving the confidence of the CEO and board has been one of my proudest achievements.

WHAT MAKES A GREAT CISO?

You should be a good salesman and change agent. Once you understand how much security's enough you need to convince people that it's the right thing to do and to pay for it—that's selling. My experience as a consultant at KPMG taught me a high standard for that.

WHAT WOULD YOU CHANGE ABOUT THE SECURITY INDUSTRY?

There's no globally recognized mark of the profession at the moment. While there are many tests of knowledge and memory, there's nothing about competence, which you need to be able to demonstrate to get the job done. If we could get to that level—such as that of doctors, accountants, and lawyers where there's a very high barrier to entry, a test of competence, a code of ethics and behavior and a strong regulator with the power to sanction and expel individuals—cybersecurity would truly become a profession that would attract the best people and that employers could rely on.

WHAT DO YOU BELIEVE THE GOVERNMENT'S ROLE IS IN SECURITY, AND WHAT ARE THEY DOING WELL AND WHAT NEEDS IMPROVING?

First, it should be about educating the population. No other institution can do this—only the government can teach across the whole population. Unfortunately, most governments do this very badly, and many people don't know how to protect themselves online. They should also be thinking about the protection of critical national infrastructure and making sure that there's adequate investment in this and in innovation. The British government has tried to do that but it still has some way to go. Governments should also be briefing corporations about the changing nature of threats and how they can defend themselves. Most corporations don't have the resources to track and monitor threat actors. However, there's a tension between the intelligence services not wanting to tip off the threat actors that they are being watched, so there's a natural disinclination for anyone from any intelligence service to communicate anything they found out in case it leaks back. That needs to change.

WHAT IS THE INDUSTRY OUTLOOK?

Threats are getting more complex, while the number of organizations that need cybersecurity functions is increasing. The original focus was in banking, then it went to critical national infrastructure like utilities and transport. Next came organizations with intellectual property like pharmaceuticals, and now it's spreading into the retail organizations, hospitality, and other organizations with large volumes of personal information.

IS THERE A NEXT STEP AFTER YOU'VE BEEN A CISO?

For some, it might be a move into a broader Chief Risk Officer or IT leadership role. I've been a serial CISO and will do a fourth role if I find a really exciting and challenging role. I have no ambition to do a broader job. Currently I have my own consultancy firm, I am a member of a number of advisory Boards, I am also continuing my research at Royal Holloway, and I do some charity work. It's certainly not the end.

8

THE FUTURE OF CYBERSECURITY

Chapter Summary

There is unique opportunity for cybersecurity professionals who want to be on the right side of things and history.

The time is ripe for those who want to take advantage of this interconnectedness, get paid well and have fun along the way.

There's no doubt that the world will continue to get smaller as we embrace innovation and become more connected. Remember the idea that we're only six degrees of separation way from each other (or Kevin Bacon)? It is the notion that anyone may be connected to another person via just five intermediaries. It sounds cool that you and I are possibly linked to celebrities or historical figures without even knowing it. But once you remember that you can now build a content marketing platform made up of blogs, videos, and podcasts to build a multi-million-dollar business, send a message to a favorite celebrity on Twitter who will share it with their gazillion other fans, or upload a dancing video of yourself quitting your job on YouTube that will be captured by BBC, CNN, Fox & Friends, and a variety of other networks, the degrees of separation are closer to four or even three.

The truth of the matter is that many of us are over-connected and things are going to get worse. We can avert some of the impending challenges by taking action now to defend ourselves and our organizations by implementing some basic cyber hygiene.

These are my top three suggestions that you can start doing today.

For companies:

1. Fix the basics before spending money on the shiny new widgets. Use the Cyber Essentials guide to assess whether you have the basics in place and then implement what's missing. https://www.cyberessentials.ncsc.gov.uk/advice/

2. Carry out risk assessments that identify the real risks and vulnerabilities in your system, and ensure that you understand what needs protecting and what doesn't need protecting.

3. Invite cybersecurity experts as non-executive directors, or the equivalent, to sit on the board and provide guidance on cyber-related issues.

For Consumers:

1. Take responsibility for protecting your own data, and do not rely on others to do it for you. (See Chapter 4 for best practices.) Find more details at https://www.getsafeonline.org/protecting-yourself

2. Insist that organizations and governments become accountable for the security of the data they hold on your behalf.

3. Think about what privacy means for you and what you want to share with everyone in the virtual space. Remember, privacy is a personal choice. Where possible request to view and delete personal data.

For Governments:

1. Be a role model and implement best practices in securing the nation's infrastructure so that companies will follow suit and protect themselves.

2. Invest in training and education for everyone.

3. Regulating our way to security is not working. In our experience this has translated to a focus on compliance and in our work, compliance does not equal security. A more radical approach is required.

Last words, career advice

There is a unique opportunity for Cybersecurity professionals who want to be on the right side of history and in a critical and flourishing industry that faces unique opportunities. The time is ripe for those who want to take advantage of the interconnectedness, get paid well, and have fun along the way. To get ahead I recommend the following:

1. You must be able to communicate with business leaders in terms they understand. You must understand the differences between business risks and tactical risks.

2. Acquire the attributes discussed in this book—the technical skills and soft skills—and be sensitive to the changing environments. Remember to listen, communicate, stay cool under pressure, manage expectations, and have a good sense of humor.

To get you started, here are some of the latest trends and technologies that will drive more cybercrime in a virtual world because everything is hackable and anyone could be your enemy.

TRENDS

Let's start with consumer trends—those areas where we all tend to want things to get faster, bigger, and better.

The Internet of Things (IoT): We're way beyond protecting home routers and into protecting home appliances—cars, thermostats, DVRs, or other internet-connected devices—in increasingly connected homes. Many of us now have internet connected security cameras in our homes to monitor our children, our home, or a babysitter's activities while we're away. But what happens if someone locks you out of your devices or your home? Or injects malware, such as the Marai botnet, to control your home router, your Netflix account, or even your toaster?

Driverless Cars: Autonomous driving has made it possible for cars to drop riders off at a specified location and pick them up later from the same spot. This new technology is loaded with communication risks—from interruptions between the car and the satellite that directs the vehicle, data leaks about personal information on the driver(s), or denial-of-service attacks—that can prevent the vehicle from operating properly. This means that a hacker can potentially stop a car and demand a ransom to get it back up and running, or if the car's 3G/4G connection isn't properly secured, interrupt communications and infect its network. But damage to the car's engine or navigational system is insignificant—just imagine the lasting and disastrous impact to the driver's life.

"In-Home" Delivery: Amazon has exceeded any of its inventors' expectations of delivering consumer goods by introducing Amazon Key—an in-home delivery service that unlocks your smart door lock, drops the package inside your house, and then relocks your door while an in-home wireless camera records the entire process. What if the technology records activities in your home or your conversations long after the delivery? Or what if it disables your Wi-Fi and camera to allow the delivery person to re-enter the home after delivery? When these concerns and other flaws were raised about the new service, Amazon issued a statement saying that such events were unlikely. If any did occur, they would be a result of Wi-Fi tampering and not Amazon software issues. Amazon promised to upgrade their software so that doors wouldn't be unlocked if the Wi-Fi or the camera was offline. Time will tell if other unexpected glitches come up.

Smart Grid Attacks: As cities adopt digitization and utomation of their electrical services, malicious hackers or social hacktivists can now infiltrate a power grid that serves tens of thousands of residents and businesses to shut it down or send the wrong signals to an entire control system architecture. If you live in the US, you may remember the Northeast blackout of 2003 that affected about 65 million people in Canada and the US, and many didn't get power back for weeks. That was a software bug. A full-on cyberattack would cause much more damage, and if you think it's just a matter of time until that happens, you'd be wrong; the US Department of Homeland Security has already accused Russia of targeting a power grid that serves sectors such as water, energy, and nuclear facilities.

Other trends that will present opportunities for cybercriminals to exploit include identity theft, wire fraud, organized crime, doxing (publishing another's private information online without their permission), child pornography, and cyber bulling.

While certain trends will play an important role in the future of cybersecurity, the key reasons this field is a growing one will remain. The growing data problem means that more of everyone's information will end up stored in the cloud and be highly attractive to cybercriminals. Consumers want products and services faster, cheaper, and better, signaling marketers to rush to upgrade and deploy new technology—sometimes with glitches—that will need future improvements. Because we don't value our privacy as much as we should, we leave ourselves open to malicious attacks. As long as our shared experiences remain interconnected and we rely on IoT-connected gadgets and devices, virtual assistants, complex systems, and connected infrastructures to conduct daily tasks, the attack surface will continue to expand in size and complexity.

In all the above examples, manufacturers will need help creating enhanced security controls, authentication, and encryption for their devices to keep hackers from accessing and communicating with them, as well as experts to analyze and report on the devices' performance.

TECHNOLOGIES

Cloud Technology: As more businesses and government agencies use cloud technology to store their data, more hackers will follow them right to their corporate cloud in hopes of accessing company information, source codes, and consumer data. This spells a growing need for virtualized systems security expertise to minimize nation-state attacks, malware injections, spear phishing, denial-of-service, and human error to name a few.

Ransomware: There are now significantly more phones in the world than there are laptops, and my prediction is that hackers will soon start locking up phones. Why? It's easy, and can be highly profitable. If someone broke into your phone and asked for $1 to unlock it, you'd probably comply because you already spent $600 to $1,000 on it. A one-trick-pony hacker can make a killing, since most of us own at least one cell phone.

Hardware Authentication: Because we are so connected at work and in business, we will need more secure ways to access networks. Hackers know that individuals often use weak passwords and need to access multiple platforms, increasing the need for more secure user authentication methods, especially in IoT setups where multiple devices share a network.

Artificial Intelligence (AI): Independent, autonomous technology that performs in the absence of human interaction is already here. It's smarter and faster than computers or humans, upgrades constantly, and flags threats faster than a patch can be deployed. But it's not perfect. Although most attacks happen without AI, humans will still need to work with AI to develop better and smarter security solutions.

Last words, concluding thoughts

By now, you have a good grasp of what it takes to enter this rewarding field, so if you're serious about pursuing it, make sure to review Chapter 6 for the next steps. You also have a better understanding of the issues surrounding privacy and online security, and that the current mechanisms just aren't protecting us. I don't know if the internet will ever be a safe place. But I know that in its current state, we all need to take more responsibility in educating and protecting our identities and everything we use online.

So, where does this leave you? I'll say it one last time: people, businesses, and governments continue to act negligently toward their own data and privacy. With some planning, you can become part of the ranks of those who help individuals and organizations of all types get it right—whether it's helping to educate them in preventing hacks, or investigating breaches and helping them recover. Although this is the end of the book, I hope this isn't the end of our time together. If you need to talk about the industry, feel free to contact me at the address below, and I'll try my best to answer your questions and help you make sense of things.

Finally I sincerely thank you for taking the time to learn more about cybersecurity. It's now time for you to take the reins and strategize on how to pursue this field, and I hope you do. While there's certainly an opportunity to be on the dark side of things, wreak some havoc, and make money we on the "white hat" side need all the help we can get. I hope to see you on the other side.

Bill Hau

bill@born2hack.life

Appendix -References by chapter

Introduction

"Digital in 2018: World's Internet Users Pass the 4 Billion Mark - We Are Social." We Are Social USA. January 30, 2018. Accessed September 08, 2018. https://wearesocial.com/blog/2018/01/global-digital-report-2018.

"What Is Cybercrime? - Definition from Techopedia." Techopedia.com. Accessed September 08, 2018. https://www.techopedia.com/definition/2387/cybercrime.

"Global Digital Population 2018 | Statistic." Statista. Accessed September 08, 2018. https://www.statista.com/statistics/617136/digital-population-worldwide/.

Oyedele, Akin. "BUFFETT: This Is 'the Number One Problem with Mankind'." Business Insider. May 06, 2017. Accessed September 08, 2018. https://www.businessinsider.com/warren-buffett-cybersecurity-berkshire-hathaway-meeting-2017-5.

Olcott, Jake. "Warren Buffett's Cybersecurity Wake-up Call - Are We Listening?" TheHill. May 15, 2017. Accessed September 08, 2018. http://thehill.com/blogs/pundits-blog/technology/333026-warren-buffetts-cybersecurity-wake-up-call-are-we-listening.

"Global $181.77 Bn Cyber Security Market to 2021 - Analysis by Type, Technology, Verticals and Applications." Benzinga. Accessed September 08, 2018. https://www.benzinga.com/pressreleases/17/10/g10185990/global-181-77-bn-cyber-security-market-to-2021-analysis-by-type-techno

Chapter 1

Finkle, Jim. "Shamoon Virus Returns in New Gulf Cyber Attacks after Four-year Hiatus." Reuters. December 01, 2016. Accessed September 08, 2018. https://www.reuters.com/article/us-cyber-saudi-shamoon/shamoon-virus-returns-in-new-gulf-cyber-attacks-after-four-year-hiatus-idUSKBN-13Q38B.

Perlroth, Nicole. "In Cyberattack on Saudi Firm, U.S. Sees Iran Firing Back." The New York Times. October 24, 2012. Accessed September 08, 2018. https://www.nytimes.com/2012/10/24/business/global/cyberattack-on-saudi-oil-firm-disquiets-us.html.

Bumiller, Elisabeth, and Thom Shanker. "Panetta Warns of Dire Threat of Cyberattack on U.S." The New York Times. October 12, 2012. Accessed September 08, 2018. https://www.nytimes.com/2012/10/12/world/panetta-warns-of-dire-threat-of-cyberattack.html.

The Radicati Group, Inc. *Email Statistics Report,* 2017-2021

Ponemon Institute, LLC., *2017 Cost of Data Breach Study*, June 2017

Newman, Jared. "Sony and George Hotz Settle PS3 Hacking Lawsuit." Technologizer. May 11, 2014. Accessed September 08, 2018. https://www.technologizer.com/2011/04/11/sony-george-hotz-settle-ps3-hacking-lawsuit/.

Tassi, Paul. "Sony Pegs PSN Attack Costs at $170 Million, $3.1B Total Loss for 2011." Forbes. August 11, 2011. Accessed September 08, 2018. https://www.forbes.com/sites/insertcoin/2011/05/23/sony-pegs-psn-attack-costs-at-170-million/#23032e9744ca.

Staff, National. "The Arab Spring Country by Country." The National. June 17, 2011. Accessed September 08, 2018. https://www.thenational.ae/world/the-arab-spring-country-by-country-1.401358.

Perlroth, Nicole, and Clifford Krauss. "A Cyberattack in Saudi Arabia Had a Deadly Goal. Experts Fear Another Try." The New York Times. March 15, 2018. Accessed September 08, 2018. https://www.nytimes.com/2018/03/15/technology/saudi-arabia-hacks-cyberattacks.html.

Pagliery, Jose. "The inside Story of the Biggest Hack in History." CNN-tech. August 05, 2015. Accessed September 08, 2018. https://money.cnn.com/2015/08/05/technology/aramco-hack/index.html.

Perlroth, Nicole. "In Cyberattack on Saudi Firm, U.S. Sees Iran Firing Back." The New York Times. October 23, 2012. Accessed September 08, 2018. https://www.nytimes.com/2012/10/24/business/global/cyberattack-on-saudi-oil-firm-disquiets-us.html.

Schwartz, Matthew J. "Sony Data Breach Cleanup To Cost $171 Million." Dark Reading. May 23, 2011. Accessed September 08, 2018. https://www.darkreading.com/attacks-and-breaches/sony-data-breach-cleanup-to-cost-$171-million/d/d-id/1097898.

Bogart, Nicole. "Timeline: How the Sony Pictures Hacking Scandal Unfolded." Global News. December 29, 2014. Accessed September 08, 2018. https://globalnews.ca/news/1734198/timeline-how-the-sony-pictures-hacking-scandal-unfolded/.

McKinsey & Company, *The Future of Consumer-Led Retail Banking Distribution*, September 2017

Chintamaneni, Prasad. "How Banks Are Capitalizing on a New Wave of Big Data and Analytics - SPONSOR CONTENT FROM COGNIZANT." Harvard Business Review. November 22, 2016. Accessed September 08, 2018. https://hbr.org/sponsored/2016/11/how-banks-are-capitalizing-on-a-new-wave-of-big-data-and-analytics.

FOXBusiness. "Equifax Hack: What We Learned." Fox Business. December 27, 2017. Accessed September 08, 2018. https://www.foxbusiness.com/markets/equifax-hack-what-we-learned.

"Equifax Now Says 8,000 Canadians May Have Been Affected by Cybersecurity Breach | CBC News." CBCnews. October 03, 2017. Accessed September 08, 2018. http://www.cbc.ca/news/business/equifax-cyber-breach-impact-1.4317381.

Mathews, Lee. "Equifax Data Breach Impacts 143 Million Americans." Forbes. September 07, 2017. Accessed September 08, 2018. https://www.forbes.com/sites/leemathews/2017/09/07/equifax-data-breach-impacts-143-million-americans/#6008843b356f.

Parkinson, Hannah Jane. "Wake Up! Amazon, Google, Apple and Facebook Are Running Our Lives | Hannah Jane Parkinson." The Guardian. May 12, 2017. Accessed September 08, 2018. https://www.theguardian.com/commentisfree/2017/may/12/wake-up-amazon-google-apple-facebook-run-our-lives.

McCandless, David. "World's Biggest Data Breaches & Hacks." Information Is Beautiful. September 03, 2018. Accessed September 08, 2018. http://www.informationisbeautiful.net/visualizations/worlds-biggest-data-breaches-hacks.

Chapter 2

"About Foundstone." Antivirus Software, Internet Security, Spyware and Malware Removal | McAfee. Accessed September 08, 2018. https://www.mcafee.com/enterprise/en-us/services/foundstone-services/about.html.

"Hacking Exposed 7: Network Security Secrets and Solutions: Stuart McClure, Joel Scambray, George Kurtz: 9780071780285: Amazon.com: Books." Amazon. Accessed September 08, 2018. https://www.amazon.com/Hacking-Exposed-Network-Security-Solutions/dp/0071780289/ref=mt_paperback?_encoding=UTF8&me=&qid=.

Chapter 3

Steinklauber, Kirk. "Data Security Defense in Depth: The Onion Approach to IT Security." Security Intelligence. January 15, 2015. Accessed September 08, 2018. https://securityintelligence.com/data-security-defense-in-depth-the-onion-approach-to-it-security/.

"Groups." Introduction and Overview - ATT&CK for Enterprise. Accessed September 08, 2018. https://attack.mitre.org/wiki/Groups.

Lewis, James Andrew. "Economic Impact of Cybercrime." CSIS | Center for Strategic and International Studies. February 21, 2018. Accessed September 08, 2018. https://www.csis.org/analysis/economic-impact-cybercrime.

Olmstead, Kenneth, and Aaron Smith. "Americans and Cybersecurity." Pew Research Center: Internet, Science & Tech. January 26, 2017. Accessed September 08, 2018. http://www.pewinternet.org/2017/01/26/americans-and-cybersecurity/.

Lord, Nate. "A History of Ransomware Attacks: The Biggest and Worst Ransomware Attacks of All Time." Digital Guardian. April 06, 2018. Accessed September 08, 2018. https://digitalguardian.com/blog/history-ransomware-attacks-biggest-and-worst-ransomware-attacks-all-time.

Cox, Joseph. "The World's First Ransomware Came on a Floppy Disk in 1989." Motherboard. April 12, 2017. Accessed September 08, 2018. https://motherboard.vice.com/en_us/article/nzpwe7/the-worlds-first-ransomware-came-on-a-floppy-disk-in-1989.

"2017 Cybercrime Report." Herjavec Group. October 18, 2017. Accessed September 08, 2018. https://www.herjavecgroup.com/cybercrime-report-2017/.

Dearden, Lizzie. "Hacking Group Claims It Took down BBC Website to Test Power before Attacking Isis." The Independent. January 02, 2016. Accessed September 08, 2018. https://www.independent.co.uk/news/media/online/bbc-website-down-new-world-hacking-claims-new-years-eve-cyber-attack-was-just-to-test-capabilities-a6793701.html.

Paganini, Pierluigi. "Anti-IS Group 'New World Hackers' Claims BBC Website Attack." Security Affairs. January 02, 2016. Accessed September 08, 2018. https://securityaffairs.co/wordpress/43235/hacking/new-world-hackers-ddos-bbc.htm.

Wright, Kristen. "5 Common WordPress Security Issues." IThemes. January 16, 2017. Accessed September 08, 2018. https://ithemes.com/2017/01/16/wordpress-security-issues/.

Chapter 4

"Innovate. Disrupt. Grow." 2017 International. Report no. 135032-G. December 2017. Accessed September 8, 2018. https://assets.kpmg.com/content/dam/kpmg/xx/pdf/2017/12/international-annual-review-2017.pdf.

Olmstead, Kenneth, and Aaron Smith. "Americans and Cybersecurity." Pew Research Center: Internet, Science & Tech. January 26, 2017. Accessed September 08, 2018. http://www.pewinternet.org/2017/01/26/americans-and-cybersecurity/.

"Equifax Hack: What We Learned." Fox Business. December 27, 2017. Accessed September 08, 2018. https://www.foxbusiness.com/markets/equifax-hack-what-we-learned.

Sweet, Ken. "Equifax Finds Additional 2.4 Million Americans Impacted by 2017 Breach." Financial Post. March 01, 2018. Accessed September 08, 2018. https://business.financialpost.com/pmn/business-pmn/equifax-finds-additional-2-4-million-impacted-by-2017-breach.

Sweet, Ken. "Equifax Collects Your Data, and Then Sells It." Inc.com. October 06, 2017. Accessed September 08, 2018. https://www.inc.com/associated-press/equifax-data-money.html.

Mastroianni, Brian. "VTech Tablet for Kids Is Easy to Hack, Experts Say." CBS News. December 04, 2015. Accessed September 08, 2018. https://www.cbsnews.com/news/vtech-tablet-for-kids-is-easy-to-hack/.

Nichols, Shaun. "VTech Hack Fallout: What Is a Kid's Privacy Worth? About 22 Cents – FTC." The Register® - Biting the Hand That Feeds IT. January 08, 2018. Accessed September 08, 2018. https://www.theregister.co.uk/2018/01/08/vtech_ftc_settlement_hacking/.

Mukherjee, Supantha, and Jim Finkle. "Digital Toymaker VTech Hires Fire-Eye to Secure Systems after Hack." Reuters. December 03, 2015. Accessed September 08, 2018. http://www.reuters.com/article/us-vtech-cyberattack-fireeye/digital-toymaker-vtech-hires-fireeye-to-secure-systems-after-hack-idUSKBN0TM1LE20151203.

Newcomb, Alyssa. "Arrest Made in VTech Toy Security Breach." ABC News. December 15, 2015. Accessed September 08, 2018. http://abcnews.go.com/Technology/arrest-made-vtech-toy-security-breach/story?id=35776252.

"Facebook, Social Media Privacy, and the Use and Abuse of Data | United States Senate Committee on the Judiciary." Meeting | Hearings | United States Senate Committee on the Judiciary. Accessed April 14, 2018. https://www.judiciary.senate.gov/meetings/facebook-social-media-privacy-and-the-use-and-abuse-of-data.

Langone, Alix. "What to Know About Facebook's Cambridge Analytica Problem." Time. April 4, 2018. Accessed September 08, 2018. http://time.com/5205314/facebook-cambridge-analytica-breach/.

Jenkins, Nash. "Mark Zuckerberg Tells Congress He's Sorry." Time. April 10, 2018. Accessed September 08, 2018. http://time.com/5235181/mark-zuckerberg-facebook-congress-testimony-sorry/.

Chapter 5

"2017 Data Breaches." Identity Theft Resource Center. Accessed September 08, 2018. https://www.idtheftcenter.org/2017-data-breaches/.

"Number of Internet Users Worldwide 2005-2017." Statista. Accessed August 08, 2018. https://www.statista.com/statistics/273018/number-of-internet-users-worldwide/.

Khosrowshahi, Dara. "2016 Data Security Incident | Uber Newsroom US." Uber.com. November 21, 2017. Accessed September 08, 2018. https://www.uber.com/newsroom/2016-data-incident/.

"Uber Admits Covering up 2016 Hack That Affected Millions | CBC News." CBCnews. November 22, 2017. Accessed September 08, 2018. http://www. cbc.ca/news/technology/uber-hack-riders-data-cover-up-1.4413154.

"Uber Says 815,000 Canadians Affected by Data Breach as Investigation Launched | CBC News." CBCnews. December 12, 2017. Accessed September 08, 2018. http://www.cbc.ca/news/technology/uber-data-breach-how-many-1.4444088.

Menn, Joseph, and Dustin Volz. "Exclusive: Uber Paid 20-year-old Florida Man to Keep Data Breach..." Reuters. December 07, 2017. Accessed September 08, 2018. https://www.reuters.com/article/us-uber-cyber-payment-exclusive/exclusive-uber-paid-20-year-old-florida-man-to-keep-data-breach-secret-sources-idUSKBN1E101C.

Cauterucci, Christina. "The Sexism Described in Uber Employee's Report Is Why Women Leave Tech-Or Don't Enter at All." Slate Magazine. February 21, 2017. Accessed September 08, 2018. http://www.slate.com/blogs/xx_factor/2017/02/21/the_sexism_in_uber_employee_s_report_is_why_women_leave_tech_or_don_t_enter.html.

Levin, Sam. "Female Uber Driver Says Company Did Nothing after Passengers Assaulted Her." The Guardian. May 01, 2017. Accessed September 08, 2018. https://www.theguardian.com/technology/2017/may/01/uber-sexual-assault-allegations-female-drivers-san-diego.

Buchanan, Rose Troup. "Former Ashley Madison Employee Claims She Made Hundreds of Fake 'alluring Female' Profiles." The Independent. August 22, 2015. Accessed September 08, 2018. https://www.independent.co.uk/news/ashley-madison-hack-former-employee-claims-she-made-hundreds-of-fake-alluring-female-profiles-as-10466900.html.

Zetter, Kim. "Hackers Finally Post Stolen Ashley Madison Data." Wired. August 18, 2015. Accessed September 08, 2018. https://www.wired.com/2015/08/happened-hackers-posted-stolen-ashley-madison-data/.

Baraniuk, Chris. "Ashley Madison: 'Suicides' over Website Hack - BBC News." BBC. August 24, 2015. Accessed September 08, 2018. https://www.bbc.co.uk/news/technology-34044506.

Goodin, Dan. "Top 100 List Shows Ashley Madison Passwords Are Just as Weak as All the Rest." Ars Technica. December 9, 2015. Accessed September 08, 2018. https://arstechnica.com/information-technology/2015/09/new-stats-show-ashley-madison-passwords-are-just-as-weak-as-all-the-rest/.

Cox, Joseph. "Ashley Madison Hackers Speak Out: 'Nobody Was Watching'." Motherboard. August 22, 2015. Accessed September 08, 2018. https://motherboard.vice.com/en_us/article/bmjqyz/ashley-madison-hackers-speak-out-nobody-was-watching.

"2017 Financial Industry Cybersecurity Research Report | SecurityScorecard." SecurityScorecard. Accessed September 08, 2018. https://securityscorecard.com/resources/2016-financial-industry-cybersecurity-research-report.

Islamchanneltv. "Asia Wired - Bangladesh Cyber Bank Heist (interview with Bill Hau)." YouTube. June 12, 2016. Accessed September 08, 2018. https://www.youtube.com/watch?v=QLRA2HPRmGU.

Gopalakrishnan, Raju, and Manuel Mogato. "Bangladesh Bank Official's Computer Was Hacked to Carry out $81..." Reuters. May 19, 2016. Accessed September 08, 2018. https://www.reuters.com/article/us-cyber-heist-philippines/bangladesh-bank-officials-computer-was-hacked-to-carry-out-81-million-heist-diplomat-idUSKCN0YA0CH.

Al-Mahmood, Syed Zain. "Hackers Lurked in Bangladesh Central Bank's Servers for Weeks." The Wall Street Journal. March 22, 2016. Accessed September 08, 2018. https://www.wsj.com/articles/hackers-in-bangladesh-bank-account-heist-part-of-larger-breach-1458582678.

Bugge, Axel. "With 4,000 Ransom Attacks a Day, Cyber Crime Threatens Financial Sector: Europol." Insurance Journal. November 09, 2017. Accessed September 08, 2018. https://www.insurancejournal.com/news/international/2017/11/09/470794.htm.

Hall, Kat. "NHS Could Have 'fended Off' WannaCry by Taking 'simple Steps' – Report." The Register® - Biting the Hand That Feeds IT. October 27, 2017. Accessed September 08, 2018. https://www.theregister.co.uk/2017/10/27/nhs_could_have_fended_off_wannacry_says_nao_report/.

Hall, Kat. "UK Hospital Meltdown after Ransomware Worm Uses NSA Vuln to Raid IT." The Register® - Biting the Hand That Feeds IT. May 12, 2017. Accessed September 08, 2018. https://www.theregister.co.uk/2017/05/12/nhs_hospital_shut_down_due_to_cyber_attack/.

"On the Internet." FBI. Accessed September 08, 2018. https://www.fbi.gov/scams-and-safety/on-the-internet.

Vijayan, Jai. "The 7 Most Significant Government Data Breaches." Dark Reading. November 15, 2016. Accessed September 08, 2018. https://www. darkreading.com/attacks-breaches/the-7-most-significant-government-data-breaches/d/d-id/1327468?image_number=1.

"Cybersecurity Resource Center Cybersecurity Incidents." U.S. Office of Personnel Management. Accessed September 08, 2018. https://www.opm. gov/cybersecurity/cybersecurity-incidents/.

"Foreign Intelligence Surveillance Act." Wikipedia. Accessed September 08, 2018. https://en.wikipedia.org/wiki/Foreign_Intelligence_Surveillance_ Act.

"Ponemon 2017 State of Endpoint Security Risk Report." Barkly. Accessed September 08, 2018. https://www.barkly.com/ponemon-2018-end-point-security-statistics-trends.

Chapter 6

"Safety & Availability (Biologics) - Bovine Spongiform Encephalopathy (BSE) Questions and Answers." U S Food and Drug Administration Home Page. Accessed September 08, 2018. https://www.fda.gov/biologicsblood-vaccines/safetyavailability/ucm111482.htm.

"Edward Snowden." Biography.com. February 06, 2018. Accessed September 08, 2018. https://www.biography.com/people/ed-ward-snowden-21262897.

Reed, Jason, Yiru Zhong, Lynn Terwoerds, and Joyce Brocaglia. "The 2017 Global Information Security Workforce Study: Women in Cybersecurity (A Frost & Sullivan White Paper)". Report. 2017. https://iamcybersafe.org/ wp-content/uploads/2017/03/WomensReport.pdf.

"2017 Cybercrime Report." Herjavec Group. October 18, 2017. Accessed September 08, 2018. https://www.herjavecgroup.com/cybercrime-re-port-2017/.

"State of Cybersecurity 2017." Defense-In-Depth. Accessed September 08, 2018. https://cybersecurity.isaca.org/csx-resources/state-of-cyber-securi-ty-2017.

"Kaspersky Lab Study: Most Women Decide against a Career in Cybersecurity before Age 16." Usa.kaspersky.com. November 8, 2017. Accessed September 08, 2018. https://usa.kaspersky.com/about/press-releases/2017_kaspersky-lab-study-most-women-decide-against-a-career-in-cybersecurity-before-age-16.

Morgan, Steve. "Women Represent 20 Percent Of The Global Cybersecurity Workforce In 2018." Cybersecurity Ventures. July 21, 2018. Accessed September 08, 2018. https://cybersecurityventures.com/women-in-cybersecurity/.

"Palo Alto Networks and GSUSA Collaborate on Cybersecurity Badges - Girl Scouts." Girl Scouts of the USA. Accessed September 08, 2018. https://www.girlscouts.org/en/press-room/press-room/news-releases/2017/palo-alto-networks-girl-scouts-collaborate-cybersecurity-badges.html.

Morgan, Steve. "List of Women In Cybersecurity Associations In The U.S. And Internationally." Cybercrime Magazine. July 21, 2018. Accessed September 08, 2018. https://cybersecurityventures.com/list-of-women-in-cybersecurity-associations-in-the-u-s-and-internationally/.

Chapter 8

"Researchers Find "simple" Way to Hack Amazon Key." CBS News. November 17, 2017. Accessed September 08, 2018. https://www.cbsnews.com/news/researchers-find-amazon-key-flaw/.

"The Great North America Blackout of 2003." CBCnews. August 14, 2018. Accessed September 08, 2018. https://www.cbc.ca/archives/the-great-north-america-blackout-of-2003-1.4683696.

Also available to download at www.born2hack.life/resources

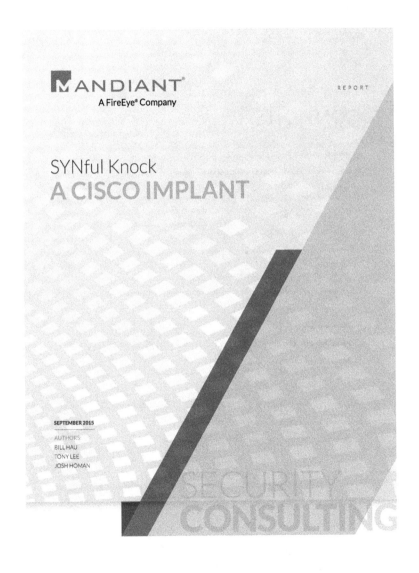

SYNful Knock   A Cisco Implant   MANDIANT

CONTENTS

SYNful Knock   A Cisco Implant   MANDIANT

Executive
Overview

Using the analogy of medieval castles, for the past 15 years we have been protecting the castle and its treasures with layered tiers of multiple large stone walls with restricted access into and out of the castle. All the while the defenders of the castle have been sitting high on the battlements trying to defend against the attacks they can see.

The fundamental assumption in this defensive strategy lies in the belief that we have dug the foundations to these large stone walls deep enough so we don't need to worry about what happens below ground. Any attack below the ground surface was deemed mostly theoretical in nature.

After the discovery of a Cisco router implant, dubbed SYNful Knock, this report will demonstrate that this supposed theoretical attack is now a reality; it will walk through the details of the compromise, impact, detection, and finally, its remediation.

We believe our findings represent the tip of the iceberg on this issue. Further research will need to be undertaken to assess the extent of the issue. In our analogy, the castle walls are akin

to the traditional legacy security technologies available, such as firewalls, proxies, IDS, antivirus, etc. The foundation is akin to the building blocks of the Internet: the enterprise router.

We already know that the large stone walls above the ground are not protecting our governments / organizations. The publicly disclosed 2015 breaches at the Office of Personnel Management OPM (USA), Kaspersky Lab (Russia), Japan Pension Service (Japan) and Carphone Warehouse (UK) are perfect examples.

As no one is really monitoring below the castle walls, we hope to reinforce the need for governments and organizations to understand that the barbarians may have already dug under the gates and they are already inside the castle.

Building a fortress on a questionable foundation does not guarantee security.

Mandiant's experience shows that this is
not just an isolated issue, but a global one.

How can this happen?

Router implants, from any vendor in the
enterprise space, have been largely believed to
be theoretical in nature and especially in use.
However, recent vendor advisories indicate that
these have been seen in the wild. Mandiant can
confirm the existence of at least 14 such router
implants spread across four different countries:
Ukraine, Philippines, Mexico, and India.

SYNful Knock is a stealthy modification of the
router's firmware image that can be used to
maintain persistence within a victim's network.
It is customizable and modular in nature and
thus can be updated once implanted. Even the
presence of the backdoor can be difficult to
detect as it uses non-standard packets as a
form of pseudo-authentication.

The initial infection vector does not appear to
leverage a zero-day vulnerability. It is believed that
the credentials are either default or discovered by
the attacker to install the backdoor. However, the
router's position in the network makes it an ideal
target for re-entry or further infection.

Finding backdoors within your network can be
challenging. Finding a router implant? Even more
so. This report not only dissects the implant, but
also provides practical methods and tools for
detecting a SYNful Knock compromise.

The impact of finding this implant on your network
is severe and most likely indicates the presence
of other footholds or compromised systems. This
backdoor provides ample capability for the attacker
to propagate and compromise other hosts and
critical data using this as a very stealthy beachhead.

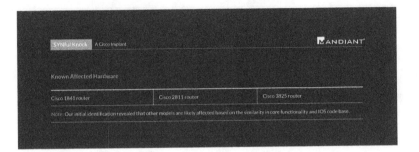

| SYNful Knock | A Cisco Implant | MANDIANT |

Known Affected Hardware

| Cisco 1841 router | Cisco 2811 router | Cisco 3825 router |

Note: Our initial identification revealed that other models are likely affected based on the similarity in core functionality and IOS code base.

Persistence

The implant resides within a modified Cisco IOS image and, when loaded, maintains its persistence in the environment, even after a system reboot. However, any further modules loaded by the attacker will only exist in the router's volatile memory and will not be available for use after reboot. From a forensic standpoint, if the modules are loaded in volatile memory, one can analyze them by obtaining a core dump of the router image.[1]

Detection Methodology

Host-based indicators are useful for organizations that can issue commands and receive the responses. This will be feasible for a small amount of routers located in easily accessible areas of the network.

Network-based indicators will assist organizations that are more dispersed or those that lack the ability to easily execute local commands and receive the responses.

Ultimately a combination of host and network-based indicators will most likely be used to determine the health of the underlying network.

Host-Based Indicators

If command-line access is possible, the following techniques can be used to detect the implant:

In addition to the command in Table 1, other detection techniques are contained within Cisco's IOS Integrity Assurance document:

http://www.cisco.com/web/about/security/intelligence/integrity-assurance.html

In the case of this implant, the size of the implanted IOS binary is the same size as the legitimate image. Thus if comparing file size, it will appear to be unmodified. Hashing the image and comparing the result to the hash from Cisco is one of the best methods to detect a modified binary; however, this will only work with an image on disk and not one that is loaded into memory.

Network-Based Indicators

Mandiant provides both active and passive network detection capabilities. A detailed description of both methods is provided below (see Network Detection).

TABLE 1: Host-based Indicator command and expected output

COMMAND	EXPECTED OUTPUT
"show platform | include RO, Valid"	Implanted router may produce no results

[1] The following blog entry shows how to produce a Cisco IOS core dump: http://blogs.cisco.com/security/offline-analysis-of-ios-image-integrity

DETAILS

Modifications to the IOS binary can be broken down into the following four functions:

1   **2**   **3**   **4**

Modify the translation look aside buffer (TLB) Read/Write attributes

Modify a legitimate IOS function to call and initialize the malware

Overwrite legitimate protocol handling functions with malicious code

Overwrite strings referenced by legitimate functions with strings used by the malware

1. TLB Read/Write Attributes

The malware forces all TLB Read and Write attributes to be Read-Write (RW). We believe this change is made to support the hooking of IOS functions by loaded modules. If the TLB attributes are not set to RW, modifications to the cached pages may not be propagated to the original page in memory.

This is accomplished with two single-byte modifications made to the IOS function suspected to be responsible for configuring the TLB. The unmodified function sets the first two bits of a register to 1, and the modified function sets the first three bits to 1. Mandiant believes that the third bit controls the Write permissions on the TLB entry. Figure 3 shows the modified instructions.

FIGURE 3:   **Modification to TLB attributes**

```
Original:
.text:XXXXXXXX 36 D2 00 03          ori      $s2, $s6, 3
.text:XXXXXXXX 36 91 00 03          ori      $s1, $s4, 3

Modified
.text:XXXXXXXX 36 D2 00 07          ori      $s2, $s6, 7
.text:XXXXXXXX 36 91 00 07          ori      $s1, $s4, 7
```

This brings us to one of the host-based indicators discussed above. The TLB attributes can be examined using the enable mode command "show platform". The TLB output of an unmodified IOS image is shown below in Figure 4.

FIGURE 4:   **TLB entries for a legitimate IOS image**

```
16M  0xX0000000:0xXXFFFFFF    0xX0000000:0xXXFFFFFF    CacheMode=2, RW, Valid
16M  0xXX000000:0xXXFFFFFF    0xXX000000:0xXXFFFFFF    CacheMode=2, RW, Valid
16M  0xX0000000:0xXXFFFFFF    0x00000000:0xX0FFFFFF    CacheMode=3, RO, Valid
4M   0xXX000000:0xXXXXFFFF    0x0X000000:0x0XXFFFFF    CacheMode=3, RO, Valid
256K 0xXXX00000:0xXXXXFFFF    0x0XX00000:0x0XXXFFFF    CacheMode=3, RO, Valid
256K 0xXXXX0000:0xXXXXFFFF    0x0XXX0000:0x0XXXFFFF    CacheMode=3, RO, Valid
256K 0xXXXX0000:0xXXXXFFFF    0x0XX00000:0x0XXXFFFF    CacheMode=3, RW, Valid
256K 0xXXXX0000:0xXXXXFFFF    0x0XXX0000:0x0XXXFFFF    CacheMode=3, RW, Valid
```

If the router has been implanted with a modified IOS image, the RW attributes should be:

FIGURE 5:   TLB entries for a modified IOS image

```
16M   0xX0000000:0xXXFFFFFF   0xX0000000:0xXXFFFFFF   CacheMode=2, RW, Valid
16M   0xXX000000:0xXXFFFFFF   0xXX000000:0xXXFFFFFF   CacheMode=2, RW, Valid
16M   0xX0000000:0xXXFFFFFF   0x00000000:0x0XFFFFFF   CacheMode=3, RW, Valid
4M    0xXX000000:0xXXFFFFFF   0x0X000000:0x0XXFFFFF   CacheMode=3, RW, Valid
256K  0xXXXX0000:0xXXXXFFFF   0x0XX00000:0x0XXXFFFF   CacheMode=3, RW, Valid
256K  0xXXXX0000:0xXXXXFFFF   0x0XXX0000:0x0XXFFFFF   CacheMode=3, RW, Valid
256K  0xXXXX00000:0xXXXXFFFF  0x0XX00000:0x0XXXFFFF   CacheMode=3, RW, Valid
256K  0xXXXXX0000:0xXXXXFFFF  0x0XXX0000:0x0XXFFFFF   CacheMode=3, RW, Valid
```

Depending on router hardware, certain ranges of memory addresses are typically read-only executable code sections. The simplest way to determine if the router has been modified is to use the "show platform | include RO, Valid" command. The IOS image may have been tampered with to allow the modification of executable code if no results are displayed.

2. Initialize the Malware
To execute the malware during IOS image loading, Mandiant believes a function associated with process scheduling was modified. This was chosen because the modified function is called early on during the IOS boot sequence, and is always called, as long as the IOS boots correctly. The target address of a function call is modified to point to the malware hook processing function. Our research has shown that the malware is initialized after the hook processing function checks whether the calling function is valid in the modified IOS. Now that the malware is up and running, it executes the original IOS function so no one is the wiser.

Mandiant believes the modified function is linked with the process scheduling task, which enters an infinite loop once called. In addition, several of the sub functions reference strings associated with process scheduling, such as "Threshold: %s CPU Utilization(Total/Intr):...".

214

APPENDIX - SYNFUL KNOCK

SYNful Knock A Cisco Implant

3. Malware Executable Code Placement

To prevent the size of the image from changing, the malware overwrites several legitimate IOS functions with its own executable code. The attackers will examine the current functionality of the router and determine functions that can be overwritten without causing issues on the router. Thus, the overwritten functions will vary upon deployment.

4. Malware Strings and Configuration

Keeping with the theme mentioned above, since the image size cannot change, the implant also overwrote some reporting strings with its own configuration. This is another indicator of compromise that can be used for detection purposes. The legitimate strings that are overwritten are shown in Figure 6.

FIGURE 6: **Strings associated with a valid function overwritten by the malware**

```
XXXXXXXX  65 63 20 00 2C 20 43 6F 6E 66 69 67 75 72 65 64   ec ., Configured
XXXXXXXX  20 49 6E 74 65 72 76 61 6C 20 25 64 20 73 65 63    Interval %d sec
XXXXXXXX  00 00 00 00 0A 4E 65 78 74 20 75 70 64 61 74 65   .....Next update
XXXXXXXX  20 64 75 65 20 69 6E 20 00 00 00 00 0A 43 75 72    due in .....Cur
XXXXXXXX  72 65 6E 74 20 74 69 6D 65 20 25 54 61 00 00 00   rent time %Ta...
XXXXXXXX  0A 49 6E 64 65 78 20 25 64 20 54 69 6D 65 73 74   .Index %d Timest
XXXXXXXX  61 6D 70 20 25 54 61 00 0A 0A 46 61 69 6C 75 72   amp %Ta...Failur
XXXXXXXX  65 20 48 65 61 64 20 25 64 2C 20 4C 61 73 74 20   e Head %d, Last
XXXXXXXX  25 64 20 4C 53 41 20 67 72 6F 75 70 20 66 61 69   %d LSA group fai
XXXXXXXX  6C 75 72 65 20 6C 6F 67 67 65 64 00 0A 54 69 6D   lure logged..Tim
XXXXXXXX  65 20 20 20 20 20 20 20 20 20 44 65 6C 61 79 20   e        Delay
XXXXXXXX  20 20 20 20 20 20 20 4A 2D 44 65 6C 61 79 20 20          J-Delay
XXXXXXXX  20 20 20 20 53 74 61 72 74 20 54 69 6D 65 73 74       Start Timest
XXXXXXXX  61 6D 70 20 20 20 45 6E 64 20 54 69 6D 65 73 74   amp   End Timest
XXXXXXXX  61 6D 70 00 0A 25 31 33 54 61 25 31 33 54 61 25   amp..%13Ta%13Ta%
XXXXXXXX  31 33 54 61 25 31 38 54 61 25 32 30 54 61 00 00   13Ta%18Ta%20Ta..
```

10

www.mandiant.com

The contents shown in Figure 6 were replaced with the contents shown below in Figure 7. Clearly visible are the malware's strings (included in the HTTP header used in Command and Control (CnC), along with the default password, which we have intentionally blanked. This will provide potential victims time to search their own networks for compromise and remediate the issue. Feel free to contact us via email at synfulknock-@-fireeye.com and we can provide the password if you suspect your system is compromised.

FIGURE 7:   **Malware strings**

```
XXXXXXXX  00 00 00 00 00 00 00 00 00 00 00 00 48 54 54 50  ...........HTTP
XXXXXXXX  2F 31 2E 31 20 32 30 30 20 4F 4B 0D 0A 53 65 72  /1.1 200 OK..Ser
XXXXXXXX  76 65 72 3A 20 41 70 61 63 68 65 2F 32 2E 32 2E  ver: Apache/2.2.
XXXXXXXX  31 37 20 28 55 62 75 6E 74 75 29 0D 0A 58 2D 50  17 (Ubuntu)..X-P
XXXXXXXX  6F 77 65 72 65 64 2D 42 79 3A 20 50 48 50 2F 35  owered-By: PHP/5
XXXXXXXX  2E 33 2E 35 2D 31 75 62 75 6E 74 75 37 2E 37 0D  .3.5-lubuntu7.7.
XXXXXXXX  0A 4B 65 65 70 2D 41 6C 69 76 65 3A 20 74 69 6D  .Keep-Alive: tim
XXXXXXXX  65 6F 75 74 3D 31 35 2C 20 6D 61 78 3D 31 30 30  eout=15, max=100
XXXXXXXX  0D 0A 43 6F 6E 6E 65 63 74 69 6F 6E 3A 20 4B 65  ..Connection: Ke
XXXXXXXX  65 70 2D 41 6C 69 76 65 0D 0A 43 6F 6E 74 65 6E  ep-Alive..Conten
XXXXXXXX  74 2D 54 79 70 65 3A 20 74 65 78 74 2F 68 74 6D  t-Type: text/htm
XXXXXXXX  6C 0D 0A 0D 0A 3C 68 74 6D 6C 3E 3C 62 6F 64 79  l....<html><body
XXXXXXXX  3E 3C 64 69 76 3E 00 00 3C 2F 64 69 76 3E 3C 2F  ><div>..</div></
XXXXXXXX  62 6F 64 79 3E 3C 2F 68 74 6D 6C 3E 00 00 00 00  body></html>....
XXXXXXXX  34 30 34 0A 00 00 00 00 00 00 00 00 00 00 00 00  404.............
XXXXXXXX  ** ** ** ** ** ** ** ** ** ** ** ** 00 00 00 00  ***blanked***...
```

Again we arrive at another host-based indicator that can potentially be used to identify the presence of the implant; however the location of the configuration strings must first be discovered and may vary depending on deployment.

A modified IOS image will produce a very different and suspicious result when running what would seem to be an ordinary IOS command. Suspicious example output is shown below:

Depending on the implant, backdoor headers may be displayed after running an legitimate IOS command.

```
<html><body><div>.3.5-lubuntu7.7
Keep-Alive: timeout=15, max=100
Connection: Keep-Alive
Content-Type: text/html
```

Backdoor Password

The attacker can utilize the secret backdoor password in three different authentication scenarios. The implant will first check whether the user input is the backdoor password. If so, access is granted. Otherwise, the implanted code will pass the credentials on for verification of potentially valid credentials. This raises the least amount of suspicion.

The following three instances were verified to enable access using the backdoor password:

TABLE 2: Authentication functions in which the secret backdoor password can be used

METHOD	PROMPT	RESULTS
Console	"User Access Verification"	Access and elevated session
Telnet	Username is the backdoor password	Access and elevated session
Elevation (enable)	Enable password	Elevated session

However, this research has shown that SSH or HTTPS sessions do not provide access for the backdoor password. This could be a configuration issue and may vary based on compromise.

FIGURE 8:   Subtle difference between authenticating using a legitimate password
              and the backdoor password

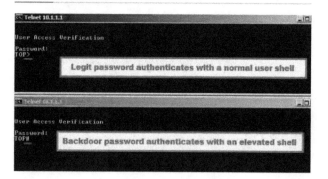

Network Command and Control

The Command and Control (CnC) portion of the implant is modular and allows additional functionality to be loaded into the IOS. The CnC functionality is stealthy because it requires a series of TCP trigger packets that the malware monitors for specific TCP header values and content. Even if filters are enabled on the router, the TCP trigger is processed by the malware. The malware will respond to trigger packets sent from three different addresses: the router interface, the broadcast IP, and the network address (the first IP in a subnet).

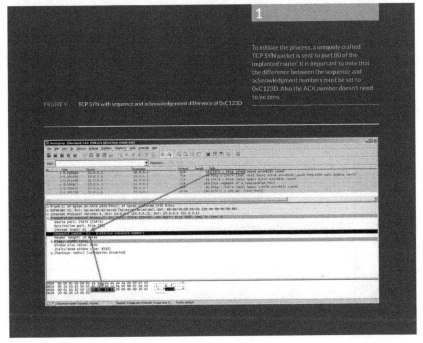

1

To initiate the process, a uniquely crafted TCP SYN packet is sent to port 80 of the implanted router. It is important to note that the difference between the sequence and acknowledgment numbers must be set to 0xC123D. Also the ACK number doesn't need to be zero.

FIGURE 9:   TCP SYN with sequence and acknowledgement difference of 0xC123D

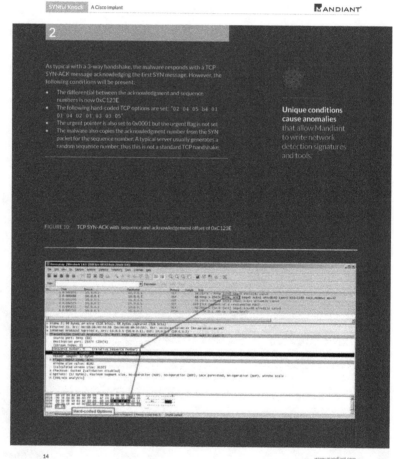

FIGURE 10:   TCP SYN-ACK with sequence and acknowledgement offset of 0xC123E

3

After the final ACK to complete the 3-way handshake, the controller then sends the following TCP message:

- The PUSH and ACK flags are set
- From the start of the TCP header, at offset 0x62, the string "text" is written
- The command shown below is at offset 0x67 from the TCP header

The command is in the following format:

`[4 byte Command Length][CMD Data][4 byte checksum]`

The [CMD Data] is XOR encoded with a static key. There is a checksum algorithm, which is a four-byte XOR of the decoded [CMD Data].

FIGURE 11:   Controller command packet

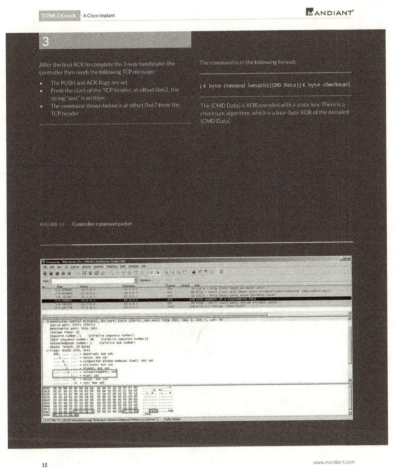

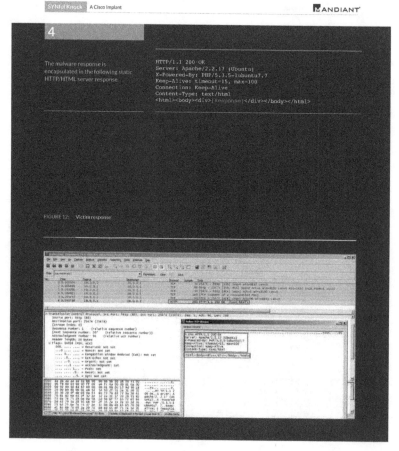

Supported Commands

We mentioned previously that this implant is modular. The five commands shown in the table below are used for loading additional modules and functionality on the victim's router. A total of 100 additional modules can be loaded; however, these modules are memory resident and will not persist after a reboot or reload.

Command messages set the first WORD (4-byte big-endian) to zero. The second WORD identifies the message type (values zero through four). All message types will start with the following eight bytes:

```
00 00 00 00 00 00 00 [00 - 04] [Optional Arguments]
```

TABLE 3: **Supported Commands**

ID	DESCRIPTION
0	**List loaded modules and their current state.** The response contains a word representing the ID number followed by a word representing the state for each loaded module. 00 - Memory is allocated 01 - Module is loaded into memory 02 - Module is activated For example, if the malware responds with this message: `00 00 00 03 00 00 02` Then, the message would indicate module 03 is in the activated state (02).

1	**Allocate space for an additional module to be loaded.** The command provides the module size for two required buffers. The malware allocates the memory for two buffers and returns the addresses in the response. The first buffer is the executable code, and we suspect that the second buffer is for configuration and storage. The syntax for this message follows this format:
	
	`[WORD ID][WORD first buffer length][WORD second buffer length]`
	
	An example command that tells the malware to allocate 0x0C bytes for the first buffer and 0x90 bytes for the second buffer of module ID 0x02:
	
	`00 00 00 02 00 00 00 0C 00 00 00 90`
	
	An example response from the server shows the first buffer is at memory address 0x66012C4C and the second is at 0x650DCD20:
	
	`66 01 2C 4C 65 0D CD 20`
	
	After executing this command, the module state is set to zero.

TABLE 3: Supported Commands continued

ID	DESCRIPTION

2	**Populate the memory allocated for the module.** This command is used to populate the executable code and suspected configuration data.
	
	`[0x80 Bytes hook data][WORD first buffer length][WORD second buffer length]`
	`[First buffer...][Second buffer...]`
	
	Similar to how the default password hook functions, the hook data buffer is used to inject additional hooks into the IOS. The hook buffer provides addresses within the IOS where hooks should be installed, and the code that should be run when the hooks are executed.
	
	After executing this command, the module state is set to one.

3	**Activate a loaded module.** The malware parses the hook data buffer and creates the necessary hooks within the OS to execute a module. The only argument is a WORD representing the module ID. After executing this command, the module state is set to two.
4	**Remove a module.** The memory allocated for the module is released and the state is set to zero. The module will no longer show up in the active modules command.

If the first WORD of a message is not zero, the code associated with the module ID of the first WORD is executed. This enables the execution of code that is not hooked into an IOS function.

Network Detection

Both active and passive network detection can be deployed to detect and prevent a SYNful Knock compromise. Passive detection can be incorporated into network defense sensors while active techniques can be used to hunt for the backdoor.

Passive Network Detection

There are a number of approaches for passive network detection. Our network detection signatures focus on four parts of a CnC session: the SYN, SYN-ACK, malware response messages and controller commands. An IDS must be able to monitor the external interface of the router to effectively detect this backdoor from the network.

1

SYN:

The first signature (included in Appendix A) detects SYN packets with the necessary delta between the TCP sequence and acknowledgment numbers. To reduce the chance of false positives, the signature assumes that the acknowledgement field is not set to zero. This signature detects probing for the malware, and does not necessarily indicate that the destination is compromised.

2

SYN/ACK:

The second signature (included in Appendix B) validates the delta between TCP sequence and acknowledgement numbers and the TCP options to detect the SYN ACK response from the malware. This signature does not assume that the acknowledgement in the SYN packet is not zero.

3

Malware response message

The signature shown below detects the HTTP server response when a command is issued. The advantage of the signature below is that it is a standard snort signature; however, it does not have the capability to validate the delta between the TCP sequence and acknowledgment numbers.

```
alert tcp any any -> any any (\
msg: "SYNful Knock Cisco Implant HTTP Header";\
flow: from_server;\
content: "HTTP/1.1 200 OK|0d 0a|Server: Apache/2.2.17 (Ubuntu)|0d 0a|X-Powered-By: PHP/5.3.5-
1ubuntu7.7|0d 0a|Keep-Alive: timeout=15, max=100|0d 0a|Connection: Keep-Alive|0d 0a|Content-Type:
text/html|0d 0a 0d 0a|<html><body><div>"; offset:0;\
flags:PA;\
sid:201504232;\
```

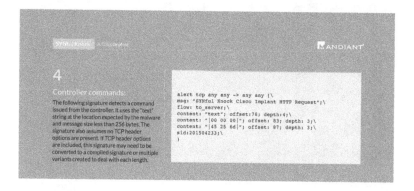

SYNful Knock A Cisco Implant   MANDIANT

4

Controller commands:

The following signature detects a command issued from the controller. It uses the "text" string at the location expected by the malware and message size less than 256 bytes. The signature also assumes no TCP header options are present. If TCP header options are included, this signature may need to be converted to a compiled signature or multiple variants created to deal with each length.

```
alert tcp any any -> any any (\
msg: "SYNful Knock Cisco Implant HTTP Request";\
flow: to_server;\
content: "text"; offset:78; depth:4;\
content: "|00 00 00|"; offset: 83; depth: 3;\
content: "|45 25 6d|"; offset: 87; depth: 3;\
sid:201504233;\
)
```

Active Network Detection

Nmap Scripting Engine (NSE)
Mandiant authored an NSE script in LUA to actively scan for the presence of this Cisco implant.

REQUIREMENTS
- Nmap v6.47 or higher (also tested with v6.49)
- Modified nselib

MODIFIED NSE LIBRARY
The NSE packet library does not allow the user to modify ack values; thus, Mandiant modified the library to allow for this capability. The diff is shown below.

```
root@nix:/usr/share/nmap/nselib# diff packet.lua packet2.lua
1013a1014,1021
>
> --- Set the TCP acknowledgment field.
> -- @param new_ack Acknowledgment.
> function Packet:tcp_set_ack(new_ack)
>   self:set_u32(self.tcp_offset + 8, new_ack)
>   self.tcp_ack = new_ack
> end
```

ESTIMATED WORST-CASE SPEED (THIS FACTORS IN HIGH UNUSED IP SPACE)

Mandiant first ran this scan using Nmap's default scan speed of -T3:

```
nmap -sS -PN -n -T4 -p 80 --script="SYNfulKnock" 10.1.1.1/24
```
Class C - 256 IP addresses (4 hosts up) - scanned in 2.29 seconds

Mandiant then ran this scan using Nmap's scan speed of -T4:

```
nmap -sS -PN -n -T4 -p 80 --script="SYNfulKnock" 10.1.1.1/24
```
Class C - 256 IP addresses (4 hosts up) - scanned in 2.28 seconds

```
nmap -sS -PN -n -T4 -p 80 --script="SYNfulKnock" 10.1.1.1/16
```
Class B - 65536 IP addresses (4 hosts up) - scanned in 2557.50 seconds (42 min)

```
nmap -sS -PN -n -T4 -p 80 --script="SYNfulKnock" 10.1.1.1/8
```
Class A - 16,777,216 IP addresses - Estimated scan time = 10,752 minutes (179 hours) = 7 days

FLAG EXPLANATION:

```
-sS = SYN scan

-PN = Don't perform host discovery

-n = Don't perform name resolution

-T4 = Throttle to speed 4

-p = port number

--script = script to execute

optional: --scriptargs="reportclean=1"  Shows the seq and ack for clean
devices too
```

Python Detection Script

Mandiant also authored a Python script to actively scan for this Cisco implant's presence. This script sends a crafted TCP SYN packet and analyzes the SYN/ACK response for indications of the implant. The script relies on the Scapy packet manipulation library (http://www.secdev.org/projects/scapy/) for processing, sending, and receiving packets. The scanning process uses several scan threads and a single thread for collecting the responses. This script is about 30 times slower than leveraging the nmap LUA script above; however, it is useful for small scans and verifying the faster scan.

REQUIREMENTS
- Python

SPEED
Class C - 256 IP addresses (4 hosts up) - 59.26 seconds
Class B - Terminated the script early due to time

COMMAND LINE

```
python ./SYNfulKnock_scanner.py -D 10.1.1.1/10.1.1.2
```

FLAG EXPLANATION:

```
-d = Target to be scanned (IP, IP/CIDR, First IP/Last IP)
```

OUTPUT

```
python ./SYNfulKnock_scanner.py -D 10.1.1.1/10.1.1.2
2015-07-14 12:59:02,760 190 INFO   Sniffer daemon started
2015-07-14 12:59:02,761 218 INFO   Sending 2 syn packets with 10 threads
2015-07-14 12:59:03,188 110 INFO   10.1.1.1:80 - Found implant seq: 667f6e09 ack: 66735bcd
2015-07-14 12:59:03,190 225 INFO   Waiting to complete send
2015-07-14 12:59:03,190 227 INFO   All packets sent
```

Nping with flags

Mandiant discovered that it is also possible to use a tool such as nping (or hping) to detect this variant of the Cisco implant.

REQUIREMENTS

- nping (installed with nmap)

SPEED

Class C - 256 IP addresses (4 hosts up) - 257.27 seconds

COMMAND LINE

nping -c1 -v3 --tcp -p 80 --seq 791104 --ack 3 10.1.1.1

FLAG EXPLANATION:

-c = count
-v = verbosity level
--tcp = TCP probe mode
-p = port
--seq = sequence number
--ack = acknowledge number
-H = (optional) Hide sent, which can speed up the scan

FIGURE 13:   Using nping to detect the backdoor

OUTPUT

```
nping -c1 -v3 --tcp -p 80 --seq 791104 --ack 3 10.1.1.1

Starting Nping 0.6.47 ( http://nmap.org/nping ) at 2015-07-14 16:08 EDT
SENT (0.0048s) TCP [10.1.1.3:37895 > 10.1.1.1:80 S seq=791104 ack=3 off=5 res=0 win=1480
csum=0xED6E urp=0] IP [ver=4 ihl=5 tos=0x00 iplen=40 id=8373 foff=0 ttl=64 proto=6 csum=0x4416]
0000   45 00 00 28 20 b5 00 00  40 06 44 16 0a 01 01 03   E..(....@.D.....
0010   0a 01 01 01 94 07 00 50  00 0c 12 40 00 00 00 03   .......P...@....
0020   50 02 05 c8 ed 6e 00 00                            P....n..
RCVD (0.0092s) TCP [10.1.1.1:80 > 10.1.1.3:37895 SA seq=3 ack=791105 off=8 res=0 win=8192
csum=0x9256 urp=0 <mss 1460,nop,nop,sackOK,nop,wscale 5>] IP [ver=4 ihl=5 tos=0x00 iplen=52
id=18496 foff=0 ttl=255 proto=6 csum=0x5d7e]

0000   45 00 00 34 48 40 00 00  ff 06 5d 7e 0a 01 01 01   E..4H@....]~....
0010   0a 01 01 03 00 50 94 07  00 00 00 03 00 0c 12 41   .....P.........A
0020   80 12 20 00 92 56 00 00  02 04 05 b4 01 01 04 02   .....V..........
0030   01 03 03 05                                        ....
```

Highlighted areas include the sequence and acknowledge numbers. The difference must equal 791102, as well as the TCP flag options described above, which must be: "20 04 05 b4 01 01 04 02 01 03 03 05".

SYNful Knock   A Cisco Implant   ᴹANDIANT

MITIGATION

After confirming compromise, the most effective mitigation is to reimage the router with a known clean download from Cisco. Ensure the new image hash values match and then harden the device to prevent future compromise. As mentioned in the overview, initial compromise is believed to occur due to either default or discovered credentials. After fixing the routers, focus on the rest of the network. If the router did not have default credentials, then the infection must have occurred some other way. A compromise assessment should follow.

APPENDIX A:
COMPILED SNORT SIGNATURE
(TCP SYN CONNECTIONS)

```
#include "sf_snort_plugin_api.h"
#include "sf_snort_packet.h"

/* declare detection functions */
int rule201504230eval(void *p);

/* declare rule data structures */
/* flow:to_server; */
static FlowFlags rule201504230flow0 =
{
    FLOW_TO_SERVER
};

static RuleOption rule201504230option0 =
{
    OPTION_TYPE_FLOWFLAGS,
    {
        &rule201504230flow0
    }
};

/* references for sid 201504230 */
static RuleReference *rule201504230refs[] =
{
    NULL
};

/* metadata for sid 201504230 */
/* metadata:; */
static RuleMetaData *rule201504230metadata[] =
{
    NULL
};

RuleOption *rule201504230options[] =
{
    &rule201504230option0,
    NULL
};

Rule rule201504230 = {
    /* rule header, akin to => tcp any any -> any any */
    {
        IPPROTO_TCP, /* proto */
        "any", /* SRCIP    */
        "any", /* SRCPORT  */
        0, /* DIRECTION */
        "any", /* DSTIP    */
        "any", /* DSTPORT  */
    },
    /* metadata */
    {
        3,  /* genid */
        201504230, /* sigid */
```

```
        1, /* revision */
    "misc-activity", /* classification */
    0,  /* hardcoded priority */
    "TCP Trigger SEQ SYN",     /* message */
    rule201504230refs, /* ptr to references */
    rule201504230metadata /* ptr to metadata */
  },
  rule201504230options, /* ptr to rule options */
  &rule201504230eval, /* use custom detection function */
  0 /* am I initialized yet? */
};

/* detection functions */
int rule201504230eval(void *p) {
    const u_int8_t *cursor_normal = 0;
    SFSnortPacket *sp = (SFSnortPacket *) p;
    uint32_t seq = 0;
    uint32_t ack = 0;

    if(sp == NULL)
        return RULE_NOMATCH;

    if(sp->payload == NULL)
        return RULE_NOMATCH;

    ack = ntohl(sp->tcp_header->acknowledgement);
    seq= ntohl(sp->tcp_header->sequence);

    if (ack == 0){
        return RULE_NOMATCH;
    }

    //Test for SYN packets
    if((sp->tcp_header->flags & TCPHEADER_SYN)&& !(sp->tcp_header->flags & TCPHEADER_ACK)){
        if ((ack > seq) && (ack - seq == 0xC123D)){ return RULE_MATCH; }
        else if ((seq > ack) && (seq - ack == 0xC123D)){ return RULE_MATCH;}
    }

    return RULE_NOMATCH;
}
```

APPENDIX B:
COMPILED SNORT SIGNATURE
(TCP SYN-ACK CONNECTIONS)

```c
#include "sf_snort_plugin_api.h"
#include "sf_snort_packet.h"

/* declare detection functions */
int rule201504231eval(void *p);

/* declare rule data structures */
/* flow:to_server; */
static FlowFlags rule201504231flow0 =
{
    FLOW_TO_SERVER
};

static RuleOption rule201504231option0 =
{
    OPTION_TYPE_FLOWFLAGS,
    {
        &rule201504231flow0
    }
};

/* references for sid 201504230 */
static RuleReference *rule201504231refs[] =
{
    NULL
};

/* metadata for sid 201504230 */
/* metadata:; */
static RuleMetaData *rule201504231metadata[] =
{
    NULL
};

RuleOption *rule201504231options[] =
{
    &rule201504231option0,
    NULL
};

Rule rule201504231 = {
    /* rule header, akin to => tcp any any -> any any */
    {
        IPPROTO_TCP, /* proto */
        "any", /* SRCIP    */
        "any", /* SRCPORT  */
        0, /* DIRECTION */
        "any", /* DSTIP    */
        "any", /* DSTPORT  */
    },
    /* metadata */
    {
```

```
3,  /* genid */
    201504231, /* sigid */
    1, /* revision */
    "trojan-activity", /* classification */
    0,  /* hardcoded priority */
    "TCP Trigger SEQ SYN/ACK",     /* message */
    rule201504231refs, /* ptr to references */
    rule201504231metadata /* ptr to metadata */
},
rule201504231options, /* ptr to rule options */
&rule201504231eval, /* use custom detection function */
0 /* am I initialized yet? */
};

/* detection functions */
int rule201504231eval(void *p) {
    const u_int8_t *cursor_normal = 0;
    SFSnortPacket *sp = (SFSnortPacket *) p;
    uint32_t seq = 0;
    uint32_t ack = 0;

    if(sp == NULL)
        return RULE_NOMATCH;

    if(sp->payload == NULL)
        return RULE_NOMATCH;

    ack = ntohl(sp->tcp_header->acknowledgement);
    seq= ntohl(sp->tcp_header->sequence);

    //Test for SYN/ACK packets
    if((sp->tcp_header->flags & TCPHEADER_SYN) && (sp->tcp_header->flags & TCPHEADER_ACK)){

        if ((ack > seq) && (ack - seq != 0xC123E)){ return RULE_NOMATCH; }
        else if ((seq > ack) && (seq - ack != 0xC123E)){ return RULE_NOMATCH; }

        //Hardcoded SYN/ACK has 6 options
        if (sp->num_tcp_options != 6) return RULE_NOMATCH;
        //MSS
        if(sp->tcp_options[0].option_code != 2) return RULE_NOMATCH;
        //NOP
        if(sp->tcp_options[1].option_code != 1) return RULE_NOMATCH;
        //NOP
        if(sp->tcp_options[2].option_code != 1) return RULE_NOMATCH;
        //SACK
        if(sp->tcp_options[3].option_code != 4) return RULE_NOMATCH;
        //NOP
        if(sp->tcp_options[4].option_code != 1) return RULE_NOMATCH;
        //Window Scale
        if(sp->tcp_options[5].option_code != 3) return RULE_NOMATCH;
        //compare the entire TCP options section
        if (memcmp(sp->tcp_options[0].option_data - 2,
            "\x02\x04\x05\xb4\x01\x01\x04\x02\x01\x03\x03\x05", 12) != 0)
            return RULE_NOMATCH;

        //All conditions satisfied
        return RULE_MATCH;
    }
    return RULE_NOMATCH;
}

/*
Rule *rules[] = {
    &rule201504231,
    NULL
};
*/
```

SYNful Knock   A Cisco Implant   **MANDIANT**

About Mandiant

Mandiant, a FireEye company, has driven threat actors out of the computer networks and endpoints of hundreds of clients across every major industry. We are the go-to organization for the Fortune 500 and government agencies that want to defend against and respond to critical security incidents of all kinds. When intrusions are successful, Mandiant's security consulting services—backed up by threat intelligence and technology from FireEye—help organizations respond and resecure their networks.

About FireEye

FireEye protects the most valuable assets in the world from those who have them in their sights. Our combination of technology, intelligence, and expertise — reinforced with the most aggressive incident response team — helps eliminate the impact of security breaches. We find and stop attackers at every stage of an incursion. With FireEye, you'll detect attacks as they happen. You'll understand the risk these attacks pose to your most valued assets. And you'll have the resources to quickly respond and resolve security incidents. FireEye has over 3,100 customers across 67 countries, including over 200 of the Fortune 500.

For more information, please contact synfulknock@fireeye.com

For more about a Mandiant Compromise Assessment from FireEye,
visit www.fireeye.com/services.html

MANDIANT®
A FireEye® Company

Mandiant, a FireEye Company | 703.683.3141 | 800.647.7020 | info@mandiant.com | www.mandiant.com | www.fireeye.com

About the Author

Bill Hau is truly passionate about defending the innocent from all the bad that is out there in the cyber world.

He has spent the past two decades immersed in the field of information warfare—assessing/breaking into computer systems and helping governments and organizations defend themselves from massive sustained cyberattacks. His mission has taken him all over the world working with different cultures across many geographical/political boundaries.

He has lead incident response teams for attacks perpetrated by a variety of threat actors, including nation states, organized crime groups, as well as hacktivist groups. Many these attacks have been reported in the world's press.

His management experience includes the building and training teams on a global scale, for organizations such as Cylance, Mandiant/FireEye, Foundstone, IBM, Internet Security Systems, and McAfee/Intel.

Bill has taught and presented at many venues worldwide, including universities, corporate headquarters, government facilities, and Black Hat (Las Vegas).